Broke the Bread, Spilled the Tea

Mitchell Kesller

Edited by
Leslie M. Ross

Illustrated by
Vick I.

Promethean Publishing Group

*To my partner who urged me never to give up,
to my aunt who paved my way forward,
and to the millions of kids out there
who love God and need to learn
to love themselves.*

Acknowledgments

This book was a passion project spanning an entire year of thorough research, of battling my insecurities, and of speaking with some of the brightest minds in the world. First and foremost, I'd like to thank my partner, Daniel, for pushing me to write beyond the boundaries of comfort. I made him suffer through multiple drafts, and he supported me each step of the way. He has been my rock and one of my brightest reasons to wake up every day and decide to keep going.

I thank my in-laws, Pearl and Tony, who covered me in constant prayer. They listened, understood, and loved me just the same. Because of the tremendous power of their prayers, I was able to push through and complete the manuscript.

Thank you to my wonderful aunts, Lis and Maria, who allowed themselves to listen to the voice of God and set the wheels of this project into motion. Their support, advice, and unconditional love have been the quintessential foundation to my journey. They taught me the virtue of perseverance even in the face of tremendous opposition.

My heartfelt thanks to Leslie, my editor, who believed in the power of this project. She took it on when so many editors before her had rejected the vision and nature of the book. It's because of her that you, the reader, won't suffer through my anxious typos and scattered thoughts. Thank you, Leslie, for challenging me to write from a place of vulnerability — you rock!

Thank you to Professor David Elmer of Harvard University.

His insight into Ancient Greek linguistics gave me the confirmation and confidence needed to tackle one of the most complicated bumps along the road. Your enthusiasm and willingness to share wisdom during our exchange displayed a passion and knowledge I rarely see nowadays.

Lastly, thank you — the reader whose support makes this project possible. I pray you will find healing in these pages and the confidence to allow yourself to be a greater ally or to be a more confident version of yourself. Your reviews of the book in the digital landscape are much anticipated and will allow this book to continue to reach thousands of lives. I highly encourage that once you finish, if you were at all touched by its contents, you pass it on to someone else who might find it to be the turning point of their own lives.

If I spoke the tongues of men and angels, if I have the gift of prophecy and can fathom all mysteries and knowledge, if I have absolute faith so as to move mountains, but have not love…

I am nothing.

(1 Corinthians 13)

Introduction

T his book was born out of a vision. Let me explain...

◆◈◆

The holiday season has always been my favorite time of the year. So much so, that on November 1st, all my decorations immediately go up — I call it, Decking Day. Bigger still is Christmas Eve, when my family gets together from across state lines to celebrate, and Christmas Day when we would spend the entirety of the day eating leftovers and playing games.

Christmas has always been a big deal for us. It was an unspoken representation of the unity we had as a family. No matter how far we would find ourselves, Christmas was *the* event where we would indulge in a time of love, laughter, and quality time with each other. Christmas of 2020 felt tremendously different.

You see, my family spans generations of highly devout Christians. As you'll find out later on in my story, there was always a pastor or church leader in every generation. For me, this was

1

both a blessing and a curse. On the one hand, I was instilled with the valuable principles of compassion, love, and the overall knowledge of God and spirituality. On the other hand, radical conservatism was zealously passed down in the bloodline, one narrow-minded parent to the next.

I've never blamed my parents for this. Their rigid upbringings made them terrific parents in many ways, but as hard as they tried, a lot of those dogmatic mindsets still lived on. None of it had ever been their fault, and I still feel extreme amounts of love for them. The moment I came out as bisexual, the reality of this news became our detriment.

My parents raised me to be a strong-headed, individualistic, and determined man. Qualities that they possess in abundance. The issue then lies in the fact that as I grew up in church, I started observing things that didn't quite line up with the teachings of Jesus, and I was *very* vocal about it. Once politics and my coming out were involved, it all went downhill.

Every moment spent together, arguments would erupt. Emotions were high, hurtful words often said, and everyone refused to *truly* listen to one another. So during Christmas of 2020, we had reached the pinnacle of our limits. But, for the sake of my rapidly deteriorating mental health, I began to distance myself.

Following a Christmas not spent with family and a short period on Christmas Eve awkwardly spent playing board games with my parents while avoiding the topic of the years' worth of emotional damage we had caused each other, I received a call from my aunt. But first, let me tell you a little about aunt Lis. She's a badass. The youngest of her sisters, she has always been a bit of a revolutionary in the family. She was also what we would consider the "black sheep."

Growing up, I never truly understood the animosity between my family and her. In my mind, her punk rock aesthetic amid a very conservative Christian family was the root of all her struggles. Imagine a punk rock icon of a woman with an undercut, gauges in her ears large enough to hold a carrot, flannel, skinny jeans, and piercings galore – that was the Lis I grew up with. It was only in my late twenties that I found out there was more to it. It turns out my aunt loved women. Who knew!? Since starting a family, her style has since mellowed out, but trust me, her wild, renegade, yet compassionate spirit is still the essence of who she is.

The discovery of her sexuality was something out of a TV episode. One day I mustered up the courage to tell *someone* in my family that I had accepted myself as bisexual. I have always been a huge family man, and not having the support of someone in the family felt like a weight all in its own.

Lis was the one I felt I could trust to expose such an enormous secret. I remember pacing back and forth in my bedroom, the palms of my hand were sweaty, and my heart beat seven times as fast as the call tone. *Just get it done,* I thought to myself, and after the initial pleasantries, I hit her with the "so... I have something I want to talk to you about." To my surprise, what I expected to be a panic attack of epic proportions turned out to be a two-sided "*coming out.*" Not only did we reveal both our secrets, but the call also doubled as a wedding invitation to celebrate her new life with her wife, Maria.

Let me just say that they have both been the very foundation of my journey today. Without them, I honestly would not have been able to navigate the arduous path ahead. I was in shock. It has always been my family's specialty to effectively hide things from each other, but this was next-level secrecy. I was happy, honored, and eternally grateful because Lis laid out the initial steppingstones for acceptance within my family. But back to our story...

On that faithful December 26th, Lis called me choked up

and in tears. She told me that God had spoken to her and had instructed her to convey a message to me. *God uses the gays?* Absolutely. Keep reading; I guarantee you'll find more surprises with every page.

God spoke to her about the struggles she faced, about the toxic beliefs that had torn our family apart. He consoled her regarding the path she had taken and regarding the groundwork she laid out for my own journey. He brought to light her past traumas and revealed that our family's toxicity was inherently wrong – but so were we.

"Wait," I interrupted, "so what does *that* mean!? What do you mean *we're wrong*?"

I suddenly felt a wave of immense dread wash over me as I waited for her response. It didn't help that, being an EMT, she suddenly had an emergency call and asked to call me later. My palms were clammy and I'm pretty sure I lost a bit of color in my face. You see, after all my research into bridging faith and the LGBT+ community, I had finally come to terms with God's love for me and had solidified my belief that same-sex attraction in the Bible had been *grossly* misconstrued.

It was a weird feeling. I felt at peace in my heart with whatever came next, but simultaneously, my mind was overwhelmed with anxious thoughts. It almost felt like I was trying to swim in the ocean during a hurricane, but I knew that panicking would only make me drown.

I've always been one to plan out my next move; however, during a year of pandemic-related misfortunes, I felt demoralized as I thought about what would be the next steps I would take if my whole belief system was flawed. I was on the edge of my seat. Eventually, she called back and broke the painful silence.

"We've wasted so much energy trying to win their acceptance, trying to convince them of things they're too stubborn to listen to," she said, "meanwhile, thousands of people in our community are committing suicide, losing faith, hating themselves... What are we doing about it?"

I was stunned. It was such an obvious concept, but I had completely missed it! Maybe I *was* wasting my time and newfound knowledge on the wrong people. I had tired myself trying to have civil discourse with my parents. No matter how much Biblical evidence I brought before them, no matter how much logic was presented, I was always immediately shut out with the ever-so-infamous line, "*we're never going to accept this.*"

Dang. Looking back, I wish I had found someone or something that could have given me the reassurance I needed to live out my life in abundance — as my genuine self. I remember spending so much time hating myself because of what I had been taught growing up. I desperately craved any sort of guidance to steer me in the right direction. So, what the hell was I doing to be the change?

"Shit," I thought to myself, unapologetically, "Does this mean I would have to come out publicly?"

Let me explain. In certain terms, I was already out. All my close friends were aware, my family also knew, but I had kept my bisexuality a secret from the general public. In part, because it's no one's business. I don't see other people having to announce that they're heterosexual, so I didn't feel obligated to report who I'm currently kissing to the rest of the world.

Then came my career. At the time, I worked in real estate. Real estate is very much a first-impression kind of job, and with a client base mainly composed of a homophobic Brazilian culture, I thought it best to keep this part of my life under wraps for the sake of my livelihood.

It truly sucks how broken our society is. It sucks that people are ignorant enough to assign your value based on who you choose to love, but I think it's essential for everyone in the

LGBT+ community to understand that we need to do what we must to keep ourselves afloat. Never be ashamed of who you are, but also realize that everyone's situation is different and that coming out is not a mandatory milestone in a young queer's life.

If coming out will put your life at risk – whether physically, in your family life, or your livelihood, then it's okay to keep things private, so as long as no one is getting hurt. Don't let anyone tell you otherwise. Coming out culture sometimes ignores the uniqueness of everyone's journey, and we've seen time and time again how dangerous that can be. If you're ready and have a safety net in place, do what you think best. In an age of social media where everyone is pressured to post out their lives, remember that keeping things private is *still* okay.

Up until now, keeping things private had been wildly successful for me, but with the revelation of my aunt's vision, it now felt selfish. My entire life had been lived around the mantra that I would like to live a revolutionary life, a life that leaves a long-lasting impression on the world, changing the lives of those around me for the better. Receiving her call woke me up to how far I had strayed from that mission.

"Anxious thoughts be damned," I decided, "I'm not a writer, but I'll do this."

So here we find ourselves: one bisexual dude and one queer/discreet/ally/parent/friend/sibling/or curious George staring blankly at each other through the pages of a book. Hi! *Awkwardly waves.*

I don't promise that these pages will be filled with eloquent text and a well-thought-out plot structure because, as I said, I'm no writer. I write this with one purpose: if I can share my God-given knowledge with at least one person whose life will be transformed, then I will, and that *one* person will make this worth it.

My goal is to lay out everything I know to be true: all my

research, the uncovered facts, and my logical thinking process so that you can form your own decisions and come to your own conclusion – to think for yourself. Regardless of the backlash, the criticism, whether people love it or hate it, if this book changes your life and reminds you of how amazing you are, it will be worth it.

I'd like to say that if you find a million and one bad reviews from angry Christians stating how I'm twisting the Word of God with disgusting filth and sodomy, then I'm doing something right – I'm riling up the Pharisees.

Before we get started, where are my manners? I was so wrapped up in the emotions of writing this introduction that I completely forgot we're still strangers! Hey! What's up? Hello! My name is Mitchell, and I will be your guide for the remainder of this trip. Please fasten your seatbelts as we may face a bit of turbulence. I know I did. We ask that you remain seated with your seatbelts securely fastened throughout the rougher parts of our journey and I promise to arrive at your destination in one piece – wherever that may be.

Chapter 1

A Battle Within

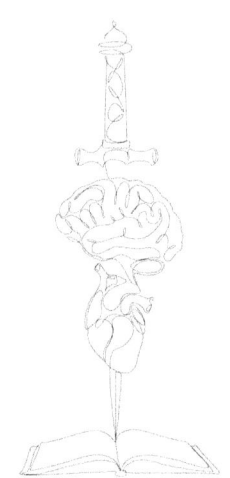

I have to be honest; I've always hated talking about myself, so don't expect this chapter to be very long. Vulnerability and public exposure of the more personal aspects of my life are all ideas that make me cringe to the very bone. I get incredibly uncomfortable when I have to open up to strangers, but I think it's important to understand the context of my past to understand where I am today. I won't bore you with details that don't matter, and I've changed names for privacy's sake.

I was born in Brazil to a family with a long pastoral history. My great grandfather was a prominent pastor responsible for creating a network of 200+ Assembly of God churches in my region of Brazil. My grandfather is a pastor who began one of the first large Brazilian churches in Massachusetts. Similarly, my uncle also started a church that became well-known in Massachusetts, of which my parents were active church leaders. Safe to say that I may as well have been a pastor's kid.

Growing up, the church was always a constant in my life. We attended services at least twice a week, and I was involved in every which way from the very start. While living in Brazil, my parents were a part of a church choir that would often travel to perform. The choir was so big and well known that they traveled across the country and even had a few vinyl records made. If you pull up any home videos of the choir, I swear to you, you will always see a minuscule human being traveling with them, singing along while doing the same exact choreography. That little creature was me!

By the time I could stand and form words on my own, I was already picking up the microphone and singing in church. I must admit, it was cute as heck to see this little minion-looking kid singing, closing his eyes, and lifting his hands in worship. God, those were simpler times!

When we moved to the United States in 1997, we kept the

same commitment to God and the church. I was an active member of the kids' ministry, heavily involved in Sunday School [Bible school], and later in life, became a worship minister, youth leader, and Sunday School teacher. I even attended college-level religious classes hosted by a prominent Christian college's satellite campus during my high school years.

One of my favorite stories in Sunday school was Luke 2:41-52. Jesus was a young boy traveling with his parents to Jerusalem for the festival of Passover. In the hustle and bustle of the thousands who caravanned to and from the ancient city, Jesus' parents lost track of him in the crowd and left him behind! When they realized his absence, they frantically returned to Jerusalem to look for him and found him seated with scholars at the temple.

> *After three days, they found him in the temple courts, sitting among the teachers, listening to them and asking them questions. Everyone who heard him was amazed at his understanding and his answers.* (Luke 2:46-47, NIV)

This story stuck with me. I wanted to be like Jesus. I wanted to learn and have the kind of knowledge that even adults would want to sit with me, amazed at how much I knew. So here I was, barely out of the toddler phase, digging into Bible stories and learning all that I could about God and the world around me. I remember I carried my illustrated Bible with me wherever I went. It became my prized possession. I was hungry to learn and still am.

By my teen years, I was already able to hold my own in philosophical and biblical debates with people twice my age, and it was honestly exhilarating. In Brazilian culture, kids/teens aren't taken very seriously, so being able to tear down belief systems, disprove incorrect concepts, or just contribute information that adults didn't know was an exciting endeavor. I loved every minute of it. This was both a blessing and a curse for someone so young because, as Spiderman's uncle Ben once said, "With great power comes great responsibility."

During those years, I was responsible for starting the youth ministry in my church. After attending a worship conference at Saddleback Church in California, I was inspired and motivated to go back to Massachusetts and implement our church's first youth service. *Amplify*, the name of the newly formed ministry, was unlike anything else in our region. Amplify outlasted my leadership and became a long-standing haven for teens to get to know God away from the judgmental eyes of adults.

Looking back, it's crazy to see how God can move in people's lives when they're away from the burden of having to perform the cookie-cutter gospel. This false gospel drives people to live in fake holiness for the sake of putting on a façade for those around them. I recognized this toxicity and tried to create a safe environment for my friends and peers while passing on the insight of who God is and how loved we are *regardless* of our imperfections. I encouraged those around me to dig into that insight and helped nurture their gifts by giving them the opportunity to lead worship, preach on stage, and explore all their talents in a new way; church roles that were generally left to the adults.

The knowledge and hunger I had for God brought about an unwanted magnifying glass over my life. Not only was I part of the pastoral family, but I became a poster child of faith for my local church community. This unsolicited role sometimes brought about a divide between my peers and me. I was often seen as "*too holy*" or "*too perfect*," though it was far from reality. This was when I truly realized the toxicity of what the modern-day church had become.

This poison made me start believing all the lies. I started to believe the narrative that God would only use me to impact peoples' lives if I fell in line with this role of holy poster child. By puberty, I was already feeling an awakening of sexual emotions towards both girls and boys, and this felt like a tarnish to my holy persona. The internal conflict set me on a dangerous spiral that I still find myself recovering from. *Cheers to religious trauma!*

From a young age, I found myself dealing with a different set of emotions. Although I had crushes on the girls in my school and was attracted to the female celebrities in the media, I found a particularly strong pull towards the boys as well. I look back and joke about how Nickelodeon's 90s TV show, Rocket Power, was my bisexual awakening.

The kids (with the horrifically ugly animation) were aspirational to me and had so many fun surfing and skating adventures that I would envy. I'm ashamed to admit, I had a crush on some of the characters; although Reggie, the girl, was dating goals for a wannabe skater like me, the main boy, Otto, had such an amazing personality that I wanted him as a *special* best friend.

I used to have imaginary adventures as a kid, and I have vague memories of imagining Otto as my secret special friend, who would sometimes sneak a kiss, or a hug, and put my friendship above all the others — a clear indicator of a part of me that I would eventually identify as bisexual. Alright... Lay off, I know it's pretty lame, but we've all had that childhood crush we were embarrassed of. The animation of the cartoon was terribly obnoxious, but hey, I was hooked!

As I write this book, the Florida House of Representatives has passed the *Don't Say Gay* bill, which aims to censor conversations of sexual orientation in schools. The terroristic rhetoric of the legislation opens up opportunities for kids to be placed in situations of severe harm if they are forced to come out to their families before they're ready. Moreover, book bans are currently happening across the nation — conservative politicians aim to erase queer literature in schools to prevent what they state, with zero expertise on the subject, as literature *aimed at influencing children's sexuality*.

Quite honestly, it's an absolute waste of time. People continuously fail to realize that regardless of censure, if a kid is gay, they will be gay. My parents sheltered me throughout most of my life from the kind of exposure that would allegedly "*turn me gay*," and yet, even as a child, these tendencies existed.

My bisexuality was never an evident part of my personality. Like I mentioned before, it's a family trademark to be good at hiding things. People are surprised when they first find out I'm bi. This has been the case throughout all my life. The only kind of bullying I truly experienced in this regard was having preferred to hang out with the girls over playing sports with the boys. This bit of information will be significant later in my story. The pressure of being the holy poster child, buying into the lie that God's work through my life was conditional, and these confusing feelings of attraction towards both sexes would later be a primary contributor to my dangerous bout of depression.

I fell in love in high school with a girl who took my breath away; we'll call her Raquel. Raquel was kind, compassionate, intelligent, beautiful, sang gorgeously, was well-liked by my parents and everyone at church, and I was determined to make her my wife – I almost did. By the end of my senior year of high school, we were engaged and later, legally married by age 22, with a ceremony to follow and marital life to become official once we finished college.

I was ready to spend the rest of my life with her, but as time passed on, I realized that maybe I had made this decision too soon. That is another major flaw of Christian culture, pushing the belief that early marriage is crucial to a person of faith, before either party is ever truly ready for it. No wonder the United States has such high divorce rates.

Our goals began to change, the direction of our lives changed, and our entire personalities evolved from who we used to be in high school. Mind you, during this time, I still wrestled with the concept of being attracted to both sexes. Nevertheless, I was ready to commit to her for the rest of my life. The love was most certainly real. However, as our character and personalities evolved, our relationship reached a breaking point where I realized we would make each other miserable down the road. I decided to do the mature thing and called things off. In my early 20s, I was filing for divorce.

As if the trauma of trying to make a failed relationship work and the pain of having to end it with divorce wasn't enough of a burden, the backlash of the church community was even greater. People who grew up with me, who I had helped minister, and had guided through some of the most challenging moments of their lives, suddenly turned their backs on me. The church took sides in a relationship that was none of its business. Mind you, this was a community of over 200 people.

This behavior wasn't limited to the youth; adults took part in the shaming as well. The behaviors from the adults in the community made it especially traumatic. Remember that one bit of information I asked you to remember? The bit about not being able to connect with the boys. Keep it fresh in your mind. We're almost there.

The end of my relationship became a Kardashian episode in the church as people started to pick sides. Shortly after, I left the church. I found it disheartening that I had spent nearly 14 years of my life dedicated to helping and loving others, only to find that this love and compassion wasn't reciprocated in my hour of need. Instead, I found cruelty and indifference. This had been the final straw that turned me away from the church community.

Once I permanently moved to Florida, I found that the same kind of disease that plagued the church community in Boston plagued those in Florida. Judgment, gossip, superiority complexes, and alienation of anyone who didn't abide by religious norms were a constant in nearly every church I attempted to become a part of. A few years later, after moving thousands of miles away from Massachusetts, I found out that people from the Boston church community were *still* rumoring as to why my relationship ended. Cue the connection of loose ends.

I was never able to form strong bonds with the boys of my community. My overprotective parents never really allowed me to hang out with friends outside of church or school, so these bonds never formed. Quite frankly, I just didn't have much in common with the guys. I wasn't allowed to play the kind of video games the boys played, I hated playing team sports, I wasn't into cars, and I couldn't get into the ordinary objectifying conversations the guys often had of girls —it's just not how I was raised. There just wasn't much that bonded me with the guys. Mix this with my peers' preconceived notion that I was *too holy* to relate to, and I was left to interact with the girls or the older crowd. This left room for speculation.

Years after cutting off communication with the people of that community and after a few disgruntled third-party events that occurred long past the end of my relationship with Raquel, I discovered that rumors were *still* circling. The tea was that I allegedly ended my relationship because of an affair I had with another man; he happened to be my best friend at the time.

Every bit of the information passed around was false and hurtful, not only to me but to Raquel as well. This infuriated me and finally opened my eyes to reality: the church does *not* practice what it preaches. Having had conversations with multiple people and observing countless different situations, I found that this is a prevalent issue beyond my own personal circumstances.

It is easy to read scripture and preach that God is love or that we should love our neighbors as ourselves, but it is an entirely different ballgame to live out what we preach. How many times have I sat in those pews and watched someone who looked different, or who was gay, or who struggled with drugs and alcohol, come into the church only to be received by judgmental glares or a cautious approach? How many times have I seen people approach them with a false sense of friendship contingent on whether they would turn away from their *"sinful behaviors?"* How many times have I seen victims of bigotry turn away from the love of God because of shame placed upon them? Shunned simply for who they are or for the mistakes they've made? I've lost count.

I understand the disdain and distrust many people have towards the church and God Himself. The actions of those who call themselves the *"people of God"* are often at the core of the issue. As Mahatma Gandhi once said,

> *I like your Christ; I do not like your Christians. Your Christians are so unlike your Christ.*

Dr. John Haynes Holmes, a Unitarian minister who spent time with Gandhi and later published his works, went on to state Gandhi's words[1],

> *I believe in the teachings of Christ, but you on the other side of the world do not; I read the Bible faithfully and see little in Christendom that those who profess faith pretend to see. [...] Their prosperity is far more essential to them than the life, liberty, and*

> *happiness of others. Christians are the most warlike people.*

I often stop and think about that quote. I've found it to be an unsettling truth. The God I've learned about throughout my entire life is a God of love (1 John 4:7-12), a God of compassion (Psalms 51:1, Psalms 103:13), a God of mercy (Ephesians 2:4-5), and a God of inclusivity (John 3:16). Why then do so many within the LGBT+ community, among others, experience similar traumas committed by the church — those who claim to be His *chosen ones*? Isn't it bizarre that the holy words of a God, preached to be loving and good, is often weaponized to bring shame and hatred?

For a long time, I struggled to separate who God is from the church. Initially, all the hurt I faced with the church led me to want to abandon God altogether. I felt as though everything I had lived was a lie. I believed God was indeed on their side, even though the church often contradicts so much of what Jesus commanded. It took a long time of quiet meditation and in-depth immersion into the Bible, long tear-filled nights with a guitar in hand and solitary worship, for me to realize that the God of the Bible isn't necessarily the God that the church portrays.

I always had a relationship with God, but as I broke up with the church, it felt like I was stuck in a situation where God was the mutual friend who took the church's side in the breakup. I guess I was still traumatized by my real-life traumas. It wasn't until a year or two after I distanced from the church community that I realized that God doesn't need to be experienced within the four walls of the church. He was so much greater than that.

Don't get me wrong, this will not be a book that bashes on the church from cover to cover. I am genuinely grateful for all that the church gave me. The principles instilled in me and the biblical knowledge that I learned while in that community, such as the value of compassion and charity, were essential in shaping me into the man I am today. When I have kids in the future, I hope to take them to church for those same initial teachings. Still, it is crucial to understand that a church is made up of humans and is thus flawed (Romans 3:23).

We all mess up; the church isn't any different. The only difference is that religion has had a history spanning centuries of being used as a weapon to declare superiority over others. We'll dive into all these different topics ahead.

Instead, the purpose of this book is to bring to light the mistakes committed by the religious, to reassure you of who God is and who He wishes to be to you. I spent most of my life thinking I was unloved by God, believing I was a mistake, something *less than* those around me. I know many of you have felt the same. My hope is that this book will be the spark needed to set aflame a lost love, or a new love, for a God who sincerely desires to be known by you.

Chapter 2

Ancient History

L et's talk about the history of the church and how it ties into our community today.

It's important to note that nowhere in the Bible does Jesus give the directive to form a physical church.[1] In fact, scripture assures us in Matthew 18:20 that if there is even two of us present in His name, in other words, to just talk about/remember/honor Jesus, He would be there too. Throughout the ministry of Jesus, we find much of the same.

At times he gave teachings at the synagogues/temples but was often seen teaching in unconventional places (Matthew 14:13-21, Luke 5:3) or at private homes (Luke 2:1-17, Luke 10:38-41). More often than not, we see Jesus living out a ministry of relationships rather than one of religiousness. On the contrary, Jesus describes his repulsion for religiousness in Matthew 23 (I suggest the Contemporary English Version translation, CEV, for easier reading.)

If we're being honest, Jesus was a bit of a party animal. He loved gatherings, food, and simply doing life with people! He was often criticized for it by the religious fanatics known as the Pharisees (Matthew 11:19). If you read more about his ministry, you'll see that the pattern was usually one of gathering, sharing, and partaking in food — living life while teaching others about God, with an occasional miracle here and there.

Jesus was a rebel by contemporary standards. He did not conform to the traditional ideas of what a holy man would look like. For example, he broke cultural conventions and spoke directly to a Samaritan woman (John 4:7-9), which was a major cultural taboo for a Jewish man. He ate and did life with sinners and tax collectors (Mark 2:13-17). He defended the adulterer who, by the law of Moses, deserved death (John 8:1-11). He existentially lived out what many today would call a radical belief system which challenged conventional norms and embraced the outcast.

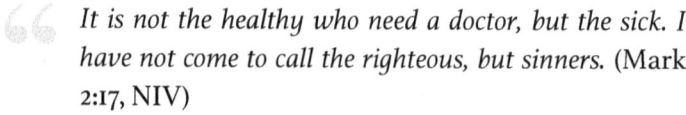

> *It is not the healthy who need a doctor, but the sick. I have not come to call the righteous, but sinners.* (Mark 2:17, NIV)

This being said, I find it hard to imagine that someone so unconventional would have the intention of setting up the exact type of establishment he so often criticized and exposed. So, what happened? Where was the disconnect here?

The Ancient Church

The ancient church is worth mentioning. What was the ancient church, you ask? This is the church that the entire Bible makes mention of. It was not a physical church where people would gather, but rather, it was varying groups of people spread across the ancient world united in their belief of Jesus. After Jesus' death and resurrection, his story was told across the the entirety of the then-known world.

Transformed by the power of such a story, people gathered together to worship and spread the belief in the Son of God. So when the Bible references the Church of Ephesus, the Church of Corinth, etc., it references the community of believers who lived in those places, *not* an organization.

The Bible has always made it clear that *we* are the church, that *we* are God's temple (1 Corinthians 12:27, 1 Corinthians 12:13, Ephesians 2:20-22) and not necessarily a physical structure. Back then, the Church would not always meet in a temple or chapel; instead, they would often meet in public spaces or private homes (Acts 19:9-10, Romans 16:5) as Jesus once did.

In the early days, the Church saw massive growth because it was a relational community. Believers would gather together to feast, to help those in need, and to listen to others share the divine revelations and instructions they received from God and the original apostles (those who actually interacted with Jesus during his time on Earth). Miracles were prevalent during this time because it was truly a "church service" not bound by time schedules, but guided by the Spirit and the needs of the people.

For some time, the Church even became an undercover operation. The Roman Empire had conquered most of the ancient world at the time of the early church. The Romans were predominantly a pagan society – worshiping Greco-Roman deities such as Jupiter and Saturn while partaking in rituals and ceremonies typical to the pagan community. This clash of polytheism against a brand-new monotheistic belief system challenged their societal structure and brought about many confrontations between them.

As more and more people converted to the ways of Jesus, the economy took a hard fall. Idol-makers, a prevalent market and profession in those times, suddenly found themselves out of business, and they weren't about to let this pass (Acts 21:19-40). Eventually, this clash of cultures would reach the highest positions of government — the Emperor. Roman Emperor Nero is considered to be the most infamous persecutor of the church in all of its history.[2] Public executions, torture, among other atrocities ordered by Nero, caused ancient Christians to go into hiding.

The very word *Christian* was initially meant to be an insult! The pagan citizens surrounding these communities of Jesus-followers began to taunt them by calling them Christians, which in the original Greek tauntingly meant *little Christs*. The insult backfired when believers took ownership of the word, thinking it a high praise to be seen as Christ-like.

Roman Imperial Sponsorship

It wasn't until Roman Emperor Constantine's rule, when it is said that he had a *"come to Jesus"* moment by means of a hallucinogenic-like vision, that Christianity was once again accepted across the Empire. It is believed that this was the birth of the traditional style of the church we see today. Sponsored and protected by most of the emperors to follow, Christian temples started to be erected to compete with pagan temples. Christianity had officially transformed from a philosophical movement to an official state-sponsored religion. Cue the messiness.

Although Constantine had a grand vision of God's power and embraced the faith himself, it is well-known that he continued with many of his pagan customs. As centuries passed, pagan traditions and festivals such as Christmas, Halloween, and even Easter became intermingled with the Christian faith to facilitate a transition from pagan beliefs to Christianity. Even the way in which Christians began to worship began to have a basis in how the pagans would worship, though scripture clearly warned against this (Deuteronomy 12:30-31).[3]

As Christianity began to overtake the known world, those in positions of leadership started to realize how much power religion had over the masses. With the fall of the Roman Empire came the Middle Ages, a time of kings and castles across the European landscape. Although many of the foundations of Roman governance and law were passed down to these newly emancipated societies, much of the Roman culture and literary tradition was lost. Christianity still prevailed, and paganism was on the brink of extinction.

Anyone with minimal knowledge of Christianity knows that

Christians base their faith on the scriptures of the Bible. What many don't realize is the history of the Bible itself. Historically, the Bible was never a single book throughout most of its written history. The word Bible simply means a collection of different books, more literally from the Latin *Biblia,* meaning books. *Groundbreaking*, am I right?

All of the books in the Bible were often written by different authors at varying points in time. The collection of books we now know as the *Bible* were originally written in Classical Hebrew, Aramaic, and an ancient form of Greek. During the Roman imperial rule, much of the Old Testament Hebrew and Aramaic were translated to Greek. It is believed this came about because many Jewish people had forgotten how to read Hebrew. This problematic situation caused Jewish leaders to quickly commission an extensive translation into the Greek language.

Since the Romans were heavily influenced by Greek society, and Greek was considered a scholarly language, many people were known to be fluent. Greek became somewhat of a standard in the Ancient world.[4] The New Testament was also written in Greek but in *koine Greek,* a version that was simplified enough for the common man and woman to understand. Koine Greek was essentially an everyday language spoken by the simple folk.

The Middle Ages

During the Middle Ages, scholars repeatedly criticized the New Testament authors' writings, stating it to be strange and almost *"dumbed down"* when compared to Plato or Aristotle's high-class writings. This was further evidence of how the founders of the *true* Church wished the Word of God to be accessible and understood by all. In the fifth century, Christian scholars *canonized,* or officially decided and established, the books to be included in what we know today as the Bible.

During the Middle Ages, as Roman influence began to subside, so did the study of these ancient languages. Soon, only the noble and priestly classes of society had the knowledge necessary to actually read scriptures – giving them unprecedented power over an uneducated population. In their hands was the knowledge needed to guarantee someone eternal life, and this was often used to the advantage of the political figures of the time.

By analyzing the history of Christianity, we see the detriment caused by the practice of withholding holy scriptures. Organized religion, to which I'll start referring to as the Church from now on (not to be mistaken with the ancient Church, as in a community of gathered believers), was responsible for the manipulation of scripture over the uninformed and ignorant masses.

This practice caused some of the greatest atrocities in history: the Holy Crusades, the Inquisition, slavery, and brutal colonization are just a few examples. Blind faith in the hands of Jesus brought about life and transformation. Blind faith in the hands of Church leaders and kings often brought about pain and destruction.

The Renaissance Era

At this point in history, Martin Luther steps in to revolutionize Christianity. By this time, the Church had become what we recognize today as the Catholic church. From its early beginnings, good intentions were often marred by human corruption. It became standard practice for the Church to demand its poor parishioners to purchase *indulgences* to guarantee salvation. In other words, for a hefty price, you too could pay to have your sins absolved, guaranteeing entry into Heaven. It sounds like a bad infomercial from your local "*Florida man*," but this actually happened.

Leaders had fooled people into believing they could buy their way into Heaven. Aside from indulgences, the Catholic church had incorporated many other practices that stemmed from the pagan roots of the Roman empire – the worship and prayer to Saints through idols or the enshrinement of the Pope as God's primary representative on Earth were all reminiscent of the many pagan gods, their idols, and the "*god-king*" Emperors of the Roman period.

Having studied the scriptures as a scholar himself, Martin Luther found many contradictions of the church in contrast to what was *actually* in the Bible. He was emboldened to challenge the Church and the Pope's power. In a power move of epic proportions, Luther nailed onto his local church's doors his 95 *theses* against the Church's contemporary practices.

His list of qualms ranged from: the unjustified act of indulgences, the unbiblical idea that the Pope had the power to forgive peoples' sins rather than God himself, the validity of purgatory from a biblical perspective (*surprise*, nowhere in the Bible does it state that purgatory exists), and whether the Pope had any control over those in it, and it further reaffirmed the argument that salvation was not through the act of works (or purchase of indulgences), but through simple faith. He wrote his theses in a way that showed he sided with the Pope, assuming the Pope had no clue what was being done and preached in his name.

Luther would soon realize that his call for academic debate over his formed theses was immediately taken as a threat by the Catholic Church. Pope Leo X was not a happy. Persecution and ex-communication [being cut off from the church, thus *allegedly* guaranteeing damnation in hell] followed after Luther refused to stand down.

Luther continued to speak on the discoveries he made in Scripture and was soon imprisoned for it. During his imprisonment at Wartburg Castle, Luther began to translate the New Testament from Greek to German – the first time in centuries that the holy scriptures were translated to the language of modern-day common men and women.[5] In his detailed notes on the process of translating, he wrote:

> *In my translation of the Bible, I strove to use pure and intelligible German. Our quest for an expression could sometimes last four weeks without us being happy with our work. (...) In addition, I have not worked on my own: I recruited assistants from everywhere. I tried to speak in German, not Greek nor Latin. But to speak German, one should not turn to texts in Latin. The house-wife, children playing, people in the street are those to learn from: listening to them teaches one how to speak and to translate – then they will understand you and know how to speak your language.*
>
> — Luther, *An Open Letter on Translating*

Like the New Testament writers who wrote in a simplified koine Greek, his goal was not to overcomplicate the Bible's language, but to write it in a way that would be accessible to anyone. With the Bible's translation came the enlightenment of the masses which led people to question the Church's wrong teachings.

That old saying that knowledge is power is genuinely one that rings true in this period of history. From the Lutheran movement came a new branch of Christianity, Protestantism, from which the many different Christian denominations of today (Assembly of God, Baptist, Presbyterian, etc.) have branched off.

Modern Day

Fast forward to today's day and age, and we find that not much has changed in the Church; it has simply expanded to the protestant branch of Christianity. I will admit, there are a few rare instances of churches who do their best to combat the natural progression of becoming institutionalized; however, as a general consensus, we find ourselves in the same situation as the Middle Ages.

The boon of Christian reformations and spiritual awakenings has *always* had three elements in common:

- a willingness to study scripture in depth,
- a desire to question and challenge doctrine for a deeper understanding,
- and a willingness to change their ways.

We saw this happen in the ancient church as people gathered to share and debate Scripture. We saw this in the Lutheran movement when people began to dig deep and question what had been taught to them as truth. Yet, in today's day and age, Christianity has become complacent.

From the perspective of the United States, where most evangelical movements have originated, Christians are lukewarm in their study of Scripture. It is an unfortunate truth that not many of those who claim to be Christian know much *at all* about the contents of the Bible. When they do, they have settled for the superficial stories once told to us as children.

I remember listening to a sermon where the pastor stated that the success of the ancient church was found in the community's hunger and desperation for more knowledge of who God is and the character of Jesus. People were actually digging into the old scrolls and finding revelations of the prophets describing everything that Jesus would eventually become during his ministry. They would excitedly bring that back to the church community and share their findings during the dinners and get-togethers they held.

People often had philosophical debates amongst themselves to better understand how Jesus would want them to live their lives, a reflection of the famous *symposiums* found in Ancient Greek and Roman cultures. Symposiums were quite literally parties held to discuss philosophy and politics among peers. These were the first *real* church services.

When was the last time you heard a sermon and researched topics mentioned by the pastor to check if they were actually true? When was the last time you took a side by side comparison of the original translation of the Bible to search for any hidden wisdom that translations may not have picked up? The reality is, not many people do.

Psychologist Tom Ward stated that humans are more likely to take the path of least resistance of acceptance based on past experiences and knowledge when faced with new information.[6] Furthermore, it is a well-known fact in psychology that humans also have a greater sense of authority bias[7] – attributing more credibility to figures in positions of authority. Mix these two together, and we get a church community that easily believes everything that is preached from the pulpit without regard to its accuracy or exploration of its content. As in the Middle Ages, we show blind faith to the leaders who claim to know the truth.

Although sometimes there may not be malice intended behind some of the superficial teachings of today's churches, it creates an atmosphere and environment of ignorance among believers. This environment takes away the critical thinking skills and analytical tools and methods needed to form the community's own sound judgment. The aftermath results in centuries-old doctrines that may not have been interpreted in the authors' original meaning, followed by believers who weaponize the interpreters' words instead of truly understanding the word of God through them.

Alright, take a breather. I know this was centuries-worth of history squeezed into a few pages. Still, it's fundamental to understand the Church's beginnings, its original purpose, and the Bible's translation to understand how it connects to the LGBT+ community.

There's still one bit of knowledge that will be important to analyze before we can tie everything up with a nice bow of understanding. It is what the Church often uses as a weapon against our community: the Bible itself.

Chapter 3

The B-I-B-L-E

The Bible has long been one of the best-selling books in the history of humanity. Its books, though ancient, continue to resonate in the lives of millions today. The biggest issue we find throughout humanity's history is our ability to take something so holy and transform it into a destructive force.

Throughout the Bible, Jesus is often seen as the bringer of life and fountain of living water (Jeremiah 2:13, John 4:14, Revelations 21:6), and he calls us to be the conduits of this living water (John 7:38, Proverbs 10:11). This theme of springs and fountains follows suit in the book of James, where James states,

> *With the tongue, we praise our Lord and Father, and with it we curse human beings, who have been made in God's likeness. Out of the same mouth come praise and cursing. My brothers and sisters, this should not be. Can both fresh water and saltwater flow from the same spring? [...] can a fig tree bear olives, or a grapevine bear figs? Neither can a salt spring produce fresh water.* (James 3:9-12, NIV)

So how can a believer who claims to preach God's love also spew hate towards another? The answer could be in a long game of telephone. I still remember my first instance of playing the telephone game when I was a kid. Funny enough, it was while I was being cared for, along with other kids, as our parents took their seminary [advanced bible school] classes. We sat down in a long line, and our nanny, Kelly, started off the game.

"Alright, I'm going to whisper a message to Mitchell, and he's going to whisper it in the ear of the next person. We'll go down the line until the last person announces the message," she explained, "don't mess this up!" I was excited. I was nervous.

This was so much responsibility for a young kid! Part of me wanted to mess it up for everyone else for pure comedic relief, but part of me wanted to make Kelly proud. Oh God, she's leaning in for the message. Memory don't fail me now!

"Please take care of my dear dog Dill, don't let him dig in the den," she whispered.

"Wait. What?" I thought to myself, "Please... take.... Care.... Of.... Something about a dog." Dang. I messed up. My young mind couldn't capture all the information at once. I turned to the next person in line, whispered an apology, and tried my best, "Take care of my dog Dill. He dug in the den."

I had never played this game. I was scared the mistake would be traced back to me! Why are my palms sweaty?! Okay, the last person is about to announce...

"Aline stole the last pieces of candy from the jar and pretended she didn't!" the last girl announced. *Well, that was definitely not what I said*, I thought to myself, feeling relieved.

Take this concept and apply it to a period spanning centuries among cultures and individuals with unique backgrounds, linguistic mannerisms, and skill levels. Regardless of the careful consideration scholars have always taken when translating sacred books, it is a statistical improbability that it would all be translated perfectly, down to the last period. Especially when it comes to ancient/Classical Greek.

Koine Greek is a language understood only by the artifacts we've found, contextual clues, and manuscripts passed down through the Middle Ages. Modern-day Greek has evolved from the ancient language, and still, most modern-day Greeks would not understand the ancient language if it were spoken to them.

Greek is a language that relies heavily on polysemy[1]. Poly-semy is the ability for words or phrases to have multiple mean-ings. In terms of a modern-day comparison, the concept is similar to our word "*run*." For example, we can run a marathon, run an errand, be running late, run away from our problems, your nose can be runny, we can run numbers, etc.

Koine Greek was no different. Many words and phrases relied heavily on contextual cues. Oftentimes they had entirely different meanings depending on external situations like the positioning in a story plot or even the time of day. Once we understand that koine Greek was also a commonplace language, it is safe to assume that slang and euphemisms may also come into play when translating.

To illustrate this, I remember being extremely confused when someone from another part of Massachusetts referred to a water fountain as a *bubbler*; it took a frustrating explanation for me to understand that people speak differently in different regions. We can assume the same in an ancient empire that melded together cultures from various backgrounds. As we break down what is known as the gay-bashing verses later on in the book, we'll see why this causes issues to the modern inter-pretation of homosexuality in the Bible.

Before we move on, let me be frank and reaffirm one thing: I do not pretend to be an accomplished theologian or a scholar of ancient languages. Instead, I am a guy who has always been deeply interested in history and a stickler for the research of credible sources — many of which I've been citing throughout this book. Since none of us were present in the times these scrip-tures were written, no one is fully able to, and with absolute certainty, interpret the specific meanings of the original authors.

This being said, while we discuss these scriptures, it's crucial that we approach and analyze them using the context of the Bible, and what we know to be the character traits of God as told by the Bible, to form logical opinions. My own determinations of these texts come from factual evidence I've researched, along with who I know God to be through His Word.

When interpreting the Bible, I approach it through the lens

of the different categories of Biblical elements: literal elements, poetic/symbolic elements, contextual elements, and historical elements.

Literal Elements

Certain scriptures mentioned in the Bible *should* and *are* meant to be taken literally. When God said, *thou shalt not kill*, it's safe to say he meant it. Likewise, when Paul writes in Romans 10:9, "If you declare with your mouth, 'Jesus is Lord,' and believe in your heart that God raised him from the dead, you will be saved," he meant it! Salvation comes when you declare Jesus as Lord and sincerely believe Him to be the son of God; no ifs ands or buts.

Poetic/Symbolic Elements

Many elements in the Bible are symbolic or poetic in nature. For example, the prophecies of the Old Testament relating to Jesus as the Messiah or Savior (known as the Messianic prophecies) were often symbolic of who Jesus would become and what events would occur:

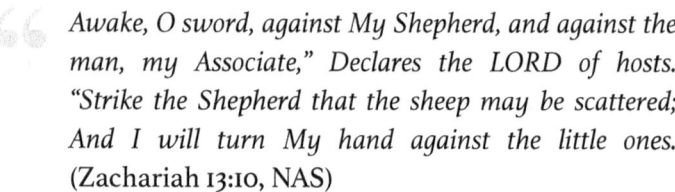

> *Awake, O sword, against My Shepherd, and against the man, my Associate," Declares the LORD of hosts. "Strike the Shepherd that the sheep may be scattered; And I will turn My hand against the little ones.* (Zachariah 13:10, NAS)

This prophecy was fulfilled in Matthew 26:56 and Mark 14:27, when the disciples scattered after Jesus' death. The verse itself was written hundreds of years earlier. Other symbolic elements are found in Psalms, a book of hymns, Songs of Solomon, a book of poetry, and in Revelations, a book believed to contain the symbolic revelation of the future.

Contextual Elements

Certain aspects of the Bible pertain to specific time periods and specific people groups. For example, the many laws handed out to the people of Israel were meant to set them apart from the other societies that surrounded them (Deuteronomy 4).

Likewise, contextual elements are essential to consider when interpreting parts of Scripture; for example, to fully understand Paul's letter to the Romans it is crucial to understand the Roman culture which highly influenced the recipients' daily lives. Without understanding contextual elements, you will never fully understand the message's meaning.

Here's a simple illustration: imagine hearing an inside joke between two people. Without knowing the background of both the joke and the two people, you will likely not understand the humor and will only be able to take it at face value.

Historical Elements

Other aspects of the Bible are purely historical records, such as the history of the Israeli people as a nation or the lineage of genealogies like Matthew 1:1-17 (that traces Jesus' ancestry to that of King David of Israel). These elements have often been proven through archaeological findings and are continuously contested for accuracy. The city of Hazor, destroyed by Joshua and the Israelites in Joshua chapter 10, was recently discovered[2] and found to have evidence consistent with Biblical accounts.

. . .

The most prevalent issue in the general Christian community is the lack of understanding of the elements necessary to interpret the Bible. We see that many people choose to take everything in a literal sense, when it wasn't written with that intention.

Today, some theologians debate whether Adam and Eve were real people[3] or if the vision, believed to have been given to Moses, was simply an allegory to mankind's creation. Likewise, it is contested that if the Bible says a day may be like a thousand years to God (2 Peter 3:8), perhaps then the creation of the universe was not done in 7 days but in millions or billions of years. To an ancient mind, the concept of billions, much less trillions, was incomprehensible.

Still, many Christians today will fight to the death to protect outdated ideals that Adam and Eve were two real people, without any valid merit, or that evolution isn't possible if you believe in Creationism. To those people I say, it is *okay* to think critically — you aren't sinning in doing so.

On a deeper and more academic level, the greatest challenge is translating meaning and accurately portraying these discoveries to the rest of the community of believers. We find this is often impossible to accomplish with a body of believers so deeply ingrained in their beliefs and indoctrinations spanning centuries.

The persecution of the Renaissance scientist, Galileo, comes to mind as a great example. At a time when the Church preached that the Earth was the center of all creation, God's greatest masterpiece, Galileo contested through scientific research that it was the sun that was centered in our solar system. When his theory was published, it caused a massive uproar in the Church. He was labeled a heretic [a person who opposes the accepted and established doctrines] and received a sentence of life in prison.

This lack of understanding, stubbornness in literal interpretation, and unwillingness to dive deeper into scriptural research is the reason the Bible is so often weaponized against the LGBT+ community. We'll explore the gay-bashing verses in the coming chapters, and I'll attempt to provide enough information for you to make your own opinions on their interpretations.

"So, you're telling me the Bible is wrong?" your mind is probably starting to argue, "but it's the word of God, you're saying God is wrong?" Absolutely not! I am a firm believer that Scripture is a direct message from God. No part of Scripture, be it the Old or New Testament, is meant to be disposed of or forgotten in terms of its message. The Bible itself speaks on this,

> *All Scripture is God-breathed and is useful for teaching, rebuking, correcting and training in righteousness* (2 Timothy 3:16, NIV)

The misunderstanding Christians find in this verse is that they equate it to mean that everything stated in the Bible *must* be taken as *absolute* truth. This isn't at all what this verse says. Let's look at the scientific method for comparison.

When scientists and scholars publish any kind of academic journals on discoveries or theories, these texts are constantly scrutinized, tested, and experimented to better understand the topic or further correct/clarify the original report. I firmly believe that the Bible was God-breathed and God-inspired, but the vessels (humans) he used to write it are not perfect beings. As such, like the scientific method, we should be continuously teaching, rebuking, correcting, and training, not only ourselves, but the interpretations of these messages as well.

Since we cannot go back and speak to the original authors and ask them *exactly* what message God gave them and how they experienced it, we can only assume through interpretation. Like our game of telephone demonstrates, this method of interpretation isn't always reliable. So the short answer is no, concepts and the message should never be disposed of but instead used with context and research to better understand how it got there and how it is meant to be used.

Scripture is meant to be studied and discussed. Without this kind of approach, the body of believers would never have reached the insurmountable numbers we see today. We study history to better understand society as it stands today; similarly, we must explore all parts of the Bible to understand God's plan for mankind.

This book is meant to be a centuries-old love story between a Creator and His beings. All of it — all the stories, verses, poems, and songs — point to one incredible end game: God's unconditional love for humankind.

That is the primary focus of the Bible and the only true reason God left instructions for us in the first place; through it, He point us to His love for us. That being said, we mustn't take such in-depth study of the Bible to the *extremes*.

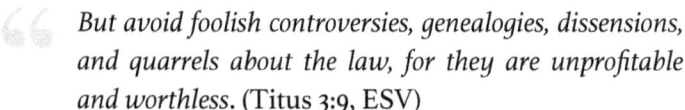 *But avoid foolish controversies, genealogies, dissensions, and quarrels about the law, for they are unprofitable and worthless.* (Titus 3:9, ESV)

Wait a minute. That sounds highly contradictory! How am I telling you that you need to study the Bible in-depth and question its interpretations, but the Bible also tells us that quarrels over interpretations are unprofitable and worthless?

The answer is quite simple. There is so much mystery and varying concepts in the Bible which can lead anyone down countless rabbit holes of debate. Its obsessive study has instigated divisions in differing opinions and even birthed conspiracy theories, such as numerology studies or arguments about what happens when we take the sacrament/communion [the bread and the wine ritual].

For this reason, many cults and sects within Christianity and Judaism have branched off in the past. People created hurricanes out of glasses of water. The best answer I can give to this is to, once again, point you to the one topic God meant to relay in Scripture – His love. Jesus said so himself,

> *Love the Lord your God with all your heart and with all your soul and with all your mind. 'This is the first and greatest commandment. And the second is like it: 'Love your neighbor as yourself.' All the Law and the Prophets hang on these two commandments* (Matthew 22:37-40, NIV)

It is truly pointless to waste time causing divisions and arguments with believers over doctrines that won't bring us any closer to God than we already are. The point I make is that open discussions and theological debate *should* be occurring with the sole purpose of leading people to a deeper understanding of God and bringing them closer to His love, not simply to argue with others.

On the other hand, if a particular doctrine or teaching tends to ostracize a group of people from His love, perhaps a closer look should be brought to the topic in question. With it, we should determine whether or not the church is genuinely teaching or acting upon it in love. As mentioned in the verse, loving God and loving people are at the core of everything God commanded. It's the overarching theme of the entire Bible.

While I was navigating through my sexuality and trying to reconcile who I was in God's eyes and in His word, I found that the topic of homosexuality did not seem to match up to the overall character of God's love. Why would God reject people simply for loving someone else of the same sex? Who is getting hurt in a loving homosexual relationship?

Don't get me wrong, I was more than willing to stick to my female attractions for the rest of my life and often prayed intensely that, if my attraction to guys was a sin, those feelings would go away. The classic *pray the gay away*. It was easier this way, for both my personal life and for acceptance into society. This request and search for a more "*normal*" self went on with absolutely no results for many years of my life.

It was always intriguing to me to consider why Jesus never once said a word on the topic of homosexuality, especially when we have a translation of the Old Testament that calls it an "*abomination*." In my mind I thought, "If it's truly so bad, why didn't Jesus say a single word about it during a time where Greco-Roman culture often embraced it?"

I started to dig deep and was highly surprised by what I found. The strong foundation that led to my questioning was found in my knowledge of who God was. Although of differing opinions on this particular matter, my parents did an excellent job teaching me the traits and character of God. Because of my deeply personal relationship with who God was, I knew something felt off — I was determined to get to the bottom of it.

I've found that, often, when those in our communities are faced with the ugly combative side of Christianity, we tend to associate that attitude with the essence of God. Wasn't He the one who ordered that sinners be stoned, and wasn't it Him who exterminated entire people groups in the Old Testament? Let's break that down by dissecting God's character in the Old and New Testament

Chapter 4

Who is God, Anyway?

F or one who states He is the beginning and the end, one not bound by time and space, God sure does have a long history. We will never know most of that history, but we can make our inferences based on the time He spent interacting with humankind.

So let's take it back to the very beginning — in Genesis. From the start, we can infer that God is a being that surpasses everything we know as the physical world. Before there was a material world, He existed. He brought the physical world into being.

> *In the beginning God created the heavens and the earth.*
> (Genesis 1:1, NIV)

From these first few verses, we find a very subtle hint as to why God created things the way he did. In verse 3, he speaks light into existence and separates light from darkness. Scientifically speaking, we understand darkness to be an absence of light. Through this act, I believe God showed us the need for contrasting elements to teach us about *potential*. I don't think it was by chance that upon creating visible light Scripture says,

> *And God saw the light, that it was **good**; and God divided the light from the darkness.* (Genesis 1:4l, NIV)

To understand light, we must have known darkness. To understand what is good, we must understand how to identify evil. What a lesson, and we haven't even left the first chapter of the Bible!

I don't believe that God created evil as many argue when speaking of things like cancer, child abuse, or catastrophes. I think our world and our existence is much more complicated than that. The evil we see in the world can never be attributed to one specific cause and effect – it's never a victim's fault. Somewhat like light and darkness, I believe that the evil we see in the world as a whole is simply an absence of goodness – an absence of God — a side effect of decisions made by humanity as a whole.

Does this mean that when bad things happen to good people, it's because God is not with them? As I said, our entire existence is too complex to place the blame, or lack thereof, on a single being; faithful believers still get cancer, innocent children still suffer, catastrophes still happen; that's just the way we see life progress.

Whether or not this proves or disproves the existence of God, I'll say this: I would rather hold onto hope (even if it's a sliver of it) than hopelessness. One day, I'm sure we'll understand the fullness of life's mysteries; I just don't think it will be while we're here on Earth.

The First Humans

After God creates the heavens and the Earth and populates it with all sorts of creatures, He decides to create humans. Up until this point, everything God created was spoken into being — His words flowed, and creation followed. However, when it came time to create humans, God took a different approach.

> *And Jehovah [one of the names of God, meaning He brings into existence whatever exists] God formed man of the dust of the ground and breathed into his nostrils the breath of life; and man became a living soul.* (Genesis 2:7, ASV)

Although we see all other parts of creation being formed by

speech, this verse aims to show us how God took his time with humans. By forming us from dust, we can simplify our visualization of this event by imagining his very own hands shaping us into form. Whether as homo sapiens, as Creationism claims, or as a distant relative in our evolutionary process is a topic for a whole different book.

Perhaps even the mere *act* of shaping mankind from the dust is an allegory to our evolution itself. Now, that's something to think about! The story continues when God then breathes his very own breath of life into us, giving us a soul. In other words, He placed a part of Himself into us. We were meant to reflect all that He is.

The Bible demonstrates how we were close companions of God. Genesis 3:8-9 gives us a glimpse of what our story with God would have been, had evil not made its way into human nature. The verses state that God was walking in the garden in the cool of the day and called out to the first inhabitants of Eden, the garden he made specifically for them.

What great company it must have been to be able to walk with God and simply talk to Him about anything face-to-face! Still, as God made the distinction between light and dark, a distinction needed to be made between good and evil. He created a single tree from which He warned the first humans not to eat. Many people tend to overlook a very subtle part of this verse.

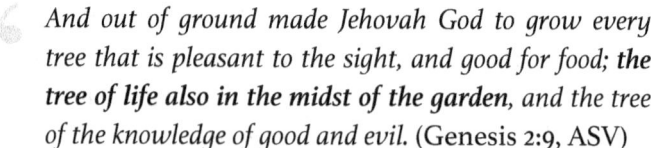

> *And out of ground made Jehovah God to grow every tree that is pleasant to the sight, and good for food;* **the tree of life also in the midst of the garden,** *and the tree of the knowledge of good and evil.* (Genesis 2:9, ASV)

When I was first made aware of this section, my mind nearly exploded. God never instructed the first humans to "not eat from the tree of life," the prohibition was only towards the tree of knowledge of good and evil. Had we chosen the tree of life, perhaps the story of humankind would have been different. Perhaps Jesus' sacrifice wouldn't have been necessary because we would have been enlightened with an eternal life with God; we would have lived without knowing suffering and evil. He gave us a choice, and we chose evil.

But why plant the tree of knowledge of good and evil in the first place? Why didn't God just plant the tree of life and let us live in eternal paradise with Him? I don't think that scenario fits into God's character of *goodness*. Imagine forcing someone to love you with no way to opt-out; is it really love if you have no other option other than to love? This is why I believe the tree was planted. God gave them the free will to either obey or disobey. We all know the story's outcome.

Okay, so they messed up. Why did God punish them by casting them out of the garden? Why didn't he just slap them on the wrists and make them regurgitate the fruit? I honestly think the first inhabitants of Eden got off easy! God could have pursued the other option: to eradicate humans altogether and start over. However, once again, that is not in God's character.

In a more reasonable and relatable scenario, consider this, most parents don't punish their children because they hate them; they punish them to teach them a lesson *because* of their love for them. Through discipline, there is growth. God loved these disloyal humans, and the love was so great, He allowed them to continue living and allowed them to grow into the billions we are today.

This perspective completely shifted my views on God and life. But let's fast forward in the Bible. Over the following years, centuries, or millennia, we see humans repeat behavioral patterns. Throughout the story of our species, humans constantly choose evil over goodness, sin over God. Sin was precisely that, a constant reminder to God that the creation He *so* loved didn't quite love Him back. The daily reminder of humanity's sins disgusted God, and soon it was like a disease spread across our kind.

What is sin? Sin derives its meaning from the sport of archery. In archery, the archer aims to shoot their arrow to a mark – be it a bullseye or any other kind of target — the goal is to hit true. If someone sins in archery, it simply means that they've missed the mark. Their arrow was shot in another direction, or it didn't hit the target it was meant for. That's all sin is. When we miss the mark of what God planned for us, we sin. A pretty impossible standard to escape as flawed human beings.

With sin plaguing our humanity, we can imagine God looking down at His creation, and instead of seeing the once pure masterpiece He formed, all He saw was the grime and filth of sin. In a powerful statement, the Bible reveals the remorse God had for creating humans:

> *When the Lord saw how great the wickedness of human beings was on earth, and how every desire that their heart conceived was always nothing but evil, the Lord regretted making human beings on the earth, and his heart was grieved.* (Genesis 6:5-6, ESV)

Cue the Great Flood.

The Great Flood

Some say it was a parable, a simple metaphor to human nature. Although we may lack physical evidence of a *global* flood in terms of archaeology, we do see geological evidence of major *regional* flooding[1] sometime during one of the Earth's ice ages. In support of this theory, it seems that numerous cultures across all continents have a version of a Great Flood passed along in their stories, with the theme often centering around the gods' displeasure with the actions of humans and the need for rebirth.

As we learn more and more about the story of humanity, we've discovered that humans may have originated from a single region before migrating across the globe. Theories suggest human life originated from Africa and the Middle East, from which we traveled and settled the 4 corners of the Earth[2]. I find it highly likely that such an impactful event in history [the Flood] could have been passed down from generation to generation into the various stories we see today.

In the story of the Great Flood, as told by the Bible, we still see evidence of God's goodness despite all the destruction. The Flood could have been the end of the human species, a chance for God to start fresh with a blank canvas, but He didn't. Even amidst all the evil of humanity, God found love for one family in particular – Noah and his loved ones.

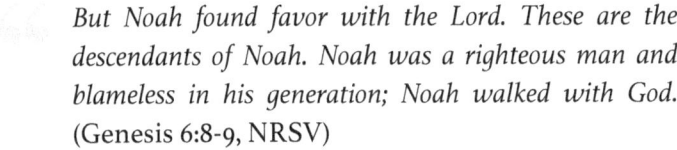

> *But Noah found favor with the Lord. These are the descendants of Noah. Noah was a righteous man and blameless in his generation; Noah walked with God.*
> (Genesis 6:8-9, NRSV)

God saw the good in Noah's heart. Justice has always been one of God's many attributes, and so it only makes sense for His justice to fall in favor with Noah and his family. Even here, God gives Noah the option of choice.

He reveals to Noah the plan for building the ark that would, in turn, save him. Noah could have rejected this plan and chosen disbelief; instead, he chose to obey. His love and obedience to God were the human species' saving grace. But what about the other innocent children living at the time? Surely it was unfair to save one family while thousands of innocents died?

Once again, I reaffirm that life and its existence are complex beyond our comprehension. As science continues to answer more and more of life's mysteries, we are often left with more questions. Researchers Rachel Yehuda and Amy Lehrner at the Icahn School of Medicine at Mount Sinai published an academic journal on the effects of traumas and psychological traits being passed down genetically from one generation to another[3].

Studies on this subject have been ongoing since the 1990s and continue to uncover evidence that these theories could play a significant factor in human development. If further experimentation proves these theories to be true, what's to say the "*wickedness*" of that previous generation of Noah's time would have passed on its traumas to the younger generations? If we start looking at the big picture of life itself, we can begin connecting the dots and make *some* sense of the questions we have about God's motives.

Once the flood had subsided, Noah, his family, and the rest of the animals on board set foot on land to begin anew. After finally stepping foot on land, Noah offered a sacrifice of gratitude to God. God was so moved by the act that He made His famous promise:

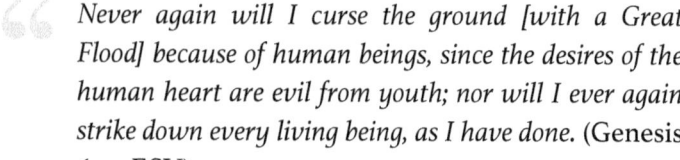

> *Never again will I curse the ground [with a Great Flood] because of human beings, since the desires of the human heart are evil from youth; nor will I ever again strike down every living being, as I have done.* (Genesis 6:21, ESV)

God knew the potential of the human heart to outshine darkness. He knew we could reflect all the good parts He originally intended for us. And so, He gave us another chance. We often see people argue about God's destructive nature, how He would order the extermination of entire people groups for one reason or another. Still, we often miss the subtle hints or the bigger picture of the original intent behind these orders. There is good in God's actions, we often miss it.

God understood that humans would always have evil in their hearts because of sin. He established rituals and ceremonies for believers to perform as a means to purify themselves before His eyes. Think of it this way: if your loved one hurts you but apologizes with flowers and chocolate, you might be inclined forgive them. It has nothing to do with the intrinsic value of the chocolate and flowers, but rather that your loved one went through a very involved process of being thoughtful to demonstrate remorse for whatever they did. Like the sacrifice of gratitude performed by Noah, these new sacrifices would serve as a symbolic reminder to God of the potential of humanity.

Even though we have tendencies towards evil, we still have good in us. This was enough for God. However, it still didn't rectify the original plans He had for us, plans for an eternity spent with him. In order to fix this, Jesus was the solution.

God sent down His only son, a piece of who He was, to perform the final major sacrifice needed for the appeasement of sin. Jesus served as the sacrifice that guaranteed our eternal life with the Creator. God sacrificed a piece of Himself, a piece of His divinity, to ensure that we'd have the option of spending the rest of our eternity with Him once again. Now *that's* a love story.

From Wrath to Grace

Here we see the shift from a God of wrath who could only see the filth of our sin in the Old Testament, to a God of grace and love who now only sees the blood of His son that was shed for us in the New Testament. When you place everything in perspective, it's hard not to feel some sort of emotion. We can quickly come to the realization of how powerful His love was for the quite literal specks of dust that we are in the grand scheme of the universe.

I believe that when people try to gate-keep who can and cannot enter Heaven based on their sin, they are indirectly blaspheming the incredible sacrifice that was made for us. When someone says to you, "you're not going to heaven because you're gay," I think they diminish the power of the blood of Jesus and completely disregard the individual's own walk with Christ – they play the part of God and not a brother or sister in Christ. So what I hear from them instead is that Jesus wasn't powerful enough to save someone *born* with same-sex attraction.

The Biblical evidence of God's character — His love, grace, and justice — goes beyond anything we could possibly understand. God punished or destroyed those with evil intentions, those who exploited others, those who caused violence and destruction, and on the contrary, always blessed those who acted in humility, love, and compassion.

Chapter 5

The Gay Bashers

Apologetics is the official term used for discourse or argumentation in defense of the Christian faith. There are courses and workshops given on the matter across all denominations. Although the average church-goer in the United States may not have studied this field of theology, most pastors or highly devout individuals will have had some form of exposure to this.

I have taken quite a few seminary workshops on the matter in the past. The purpose of apologetics is to be knowledgeable enough on Biblical concepts to readily defend the faith when it is brought into question. Unfortunately, many Christians take the principle of apologetics and weaponize it. Peter makes mention of the concept of apologetics in the Bible,

> *But in your hearts honor Christ the Lord as holy, always being prepared to make a defense to anyone who asks you for a reason for the hope that is in you; yet do it with gentleness and respect,* (1 Peter 3:15, ESV)

In other words, apologetics are solely meant for the *defense* of the Christian faith, and when it is used, it must be used with *gentleness and respect*, something we don't often see when the Church clashes with the LGBT+ community.

As we dissect the gay-bashing verses, I urge you to keep this same approach in mind. We will read the verse, analyze the Church's perspective, and further break down the verse as a defense for the queer Christian.

Do not use these explanations as weapons against others but use them to further civil discourse – with gentleness and respect. I hope you will find healing in the following pages, if you haven't started to feel it already, and I hope it gives you peace in who God is to you and, even more importantly, who you are to Him.

Sodom and Gomorrah – Genesis 19:1–11

The story of Sodom and Gomorrah is one often used to condemn homosexuality. In this story, two angels show up in human form to the notoriously sinful cities of Sodom and Gomorrah. Lot, a righteous man (who was also the famous Abraham's nephew), settled in this Mesopotamian city with his family knowing fully well of the city's sinful nature. In Islamic tradition, it was claimed that Abraham sent Lot to this city in an effort to provide testimony of God to its wicked residents.

Before moving on, we need to understand some context. In Jewish culture, hospitality is not only a kind act but a divine mandate that stems from Abraham's custom of inviting strangers into his tent (nomadic people back in those times would live in large, outstretched tents with all their family members and servants).

In Jewish theological circles, it is believed that Abraham would leave the 4 entrances of his tent wide open to invite strangers in for his hospitality[1]. Later in the Bible, this custom of hospitality would turn into a sacred mandate as referenced in Leviticus 19:33-34.

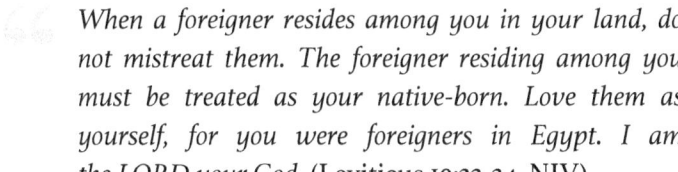

> *When a foreigner resides among you in your land, do not mistreat them. The foreigner residing among you must be treated as your native-born. Love them as yourself, for you were foreigners in Egypt. I am the LORD your God.* (Leviticus 19:33-34, NIV)

This principle is also demonstrated and held in high regard in the New Testament,

> *Do not forget to show hospitality to strangers, for by so doing some people have shown hospitality to angels without knowing it.* (Hebrews 13:2, NIV)

Leviticus is widely known to be a book of laws established by God to the people of Israel to set them apart, or *sanctify* them, from the surrounding nations of pagans. This particular mandate was important because the Mesopotamians, Hittites, and all the other subcultures within the two powers in the area, were not the kindest to strangers in their lands.

In his academic journal entitled, Foreigners in the Ancient Near East, Gary Beckman writes of many prominent figures in those ancient cultures, often belittling and mocking the customs of neighboring nations[2]. Beckman begins explaining with this statement,

> *To begin our survey with foreigners as groups located—as is only meet—within their own countries, we may observe that the Mesopotamians and the Hittites could find the ways of others somewhat distasteful.* (Journal of the American Oriental Society 133.2 [2013] pg 204.)

Although these Pagan cultures tolerated the inevitable immigration of different people groups and offered protection to those who could provide an economic benefit (i.e. merchants), the overall feeling was one that foreigners were tolerated but not welcomed. You will see why it is so essential to understand the context of the times when analyzing our original story.

It was getting to be very late in the day, and Lot immediately recognized the strangers hanging around the town square as foreigners (little did he know, these were angels in disguise, taking on human form). Knowing that they would not be safe by nighttime, he insists they come back home with him. The strangers politely decline and offer to sleep in the town square, but Lot's insistence is so strong they eventually follow him home and accept his gracious hospitality.

Word gets out that Lot is harboring foreigners in his home, and the morally corrupt residents of Sodom and Gomorrah then gather around Lot's house in droves. They would chant and demand that he turn over these strangers so they may rape them. Was it simply a matter that these residents were evil and immoral? Was it because this particular region had a stronger-still dislike for foreigners? Maybe these angels took the form of humans that would typically never be found in this area and were considered an especially prized form of conquest. We will never understand the specifics because they were never explicitly stated. Still, all these factors could have played a valid part in explaining why the residents were hellbent on raping these two strangers to their land.

Lot had an obligation by his customs and divine belief to protect these foreigners, at all costs, so as long as they were guests under his roof. If he turned them over to harm, his land, family, and goods would be cursed for as long as he lived. In desperation, Lot attempted to deescalate and did what many of us would find unthinkable,

> *Lot went outside to meet them and shut the door behind him and said, 'No, my friends. Don't do this wicked thing. Look, I have two daughters who have never slept with a man. Let me bring them out to you, and you can do what you like with them. But don't do anything to these men, for they have come under the protection of my roof.' 'Get out of our way,' they replied. 'This fellow came here as a foreigner, and now he wants to play the judge! We'll treat you worse than them. [Once again*

> *showing the locals' distaste for foreigners]' They kept*
> *bringing pressure on Lot and moved forward to break*
> *down the door.* (Leviticus 19:6-9, ESV)

So the story goes that by this point, the angels had seen enough. They pulled Lot back into the house before he faced any more harm and blinded all the men outside so they could not find the home's entrance. The angels went on to confirm whether all the family members were present in Lot's household and commanded that he take all of them and run out of the city – warning them not to look back at what was about to happen.

As Lot and his family fled the city, the angels proceeded to bring down fire from the heavens, destroying everything and everyone in these cities filled with immorality. It was during this moment that, whether by curiosity or a longing for her old life, Lot's wife turns back to look at the destruction and is immediately turned into a pillar of salt.

Because I'm a nerd for these things, I dug into the scientific possibility of this salty transformation and was surprised to find discussions stating that science could very well corroborate this unusual event. In highly simplified terms, an explosion that is both strong and hot enough to occur in a short period of time can cause the human body to quickly calcify (or look pretty salty to an ancient mind) at a relatively quick pace[3]. Read *The chemical death of Lot's wife: discussion paper*, by I M Klotz, PhD for a more detailed analysis.

In conclusion to the story of Sodom and Gomorrah, it was never about homosexuality. It was always about the immorality, racism, nationalism, attempted rape, and assertion of power over another that caused God to finally bring about the destruction of an evil society. Scary how we see these kinds of parallels in the society we live in today. Still, as long as there is at least one

Lot in the midst of an evil population, God will always show mercy and compassion.

When Christians weaponize this verse against the LGBT+ community, the only element they seem to focus on is the fact that the residents of the city were men who wished to have sex with the angels manifested in male form. It is interesting to note that they don't even give proper acknowledgement to the rape aspect of the story but instead look only to the *men having sex with men* portion.Still even from their perspective and logic, this verse was *not* about homosexuality, the moral damnation is *specifically* centered around the residents' desire to rape and exploit the foreigners.

If Christians hope to get anywhere past a superficial under-standing of God's word, they need to surrender their simplistic views and literal interpretations of the Bible and dive deeper intro true understanding. As we learned, the Bible was not written in English or in any modern-day language, so we need to stop interpreting scripture based solely off our modern-day semantics.

Bite Sized Summary
Sodom and Gomorrah

THE CHURCH'S CRUMBS: Sodom and Gomorrah had many sins, but the primary sin demonstrated here was homosexuality. All the male residents wished to rape the angels in male form and refused to rape the daughters of Lot. This clearly illustrates why God disapproves of acts of homosexuality, and it was the final straw that brought about the destruction of the cities.

SPILLING THE TEA: The actual sin here was the residents' hatred and violence towards foreigners and their desire to assert their dominance through rape, no matter the cost. This lust for abusive power over others and the evil intentions of their collective hearts, among other countless sins of injustice, was the ultimate downfall of the cities.

Leviticus 18:22

At first glance, Leviticus 18 is probably the most direct gay-bashing verse in the Bible. It is usually the verse that is most used against the LGBT+ community as a means of *"biblical proof"* of the immorality of homosexuality:

> *"Thou shalt not lie with mankind, as with womankind:*
> *it is an abomination."* (Leviticus 18:22)

I believe there is a big issue of context here. The key factor that contests the reasoning behind this verse is found in the very introduction of chapter 18.

> *And the Lord spoke to Moses, saying, 'Speak to the*
> *people of Israel and say to them, I am the Lord your*
> *God. You shall not do as they do in the land of Egypt,*
> *where you lived, and you shall not do as they do in the*
> *land of Canaan, to which I am bringing you. You shall*
> *not walk in their statutes. You shall follow my rules and*
> *keep my statutes and walk in them. I am the Lord your*
> *God.'* (Leviticus 18:1- 4, ESV)

The introduction to these sets of divine laws and decrees specifically shows their reasoning. God had always wanted to keep his people set apart from their neighboring counterparts throughout the Old Testament. He tried to establish the Jewish people as a sort of "*city on a hill*" that would differentiate them from their neighbors for their customs and traditions as God's People.

Let's pause and look at the timeline of when this book was written. When Moses [allegedly] wrote Leviticus, the Jewish people had only recently achieved a status of sovereign freedom. They had recently left the bondage of slavery in the highly pagan kingdom of Egypt and were now staking their claim in the even more pagan lands of Canaan.

Throughout their journey of deliverance in the desert, we see how easily swayed the Israelites were in adopting pagan rituals when things didn't quite go the way they expected. For example, in Exodus 32, when Moses climbed Mount Sinai for direct guidance from God on the nation's next steps, he was gone for so long that the people started to think he died.

In response to their fear of losing their leader, the Jewish people erected a golden statue of a calf to worship and ask for guidance. If there is one thing that God won't take lightly, it's the worshipping of idols before Him. So it's no wonder why decrees such as these were necessary to keep the Jewish people from straying from God.

Continuing with our train of logic, Leviticus 18 verse 3 emphasizes our rebuttal pretty nicely. The purpose of these laws and decrees was so the Jewish people would not adopt the customs of the Egyptian nor Canaanites pagans, many of whose practices involved incest, ritualistic prostitution, human sacrifices, and bestiality as a form of worship to their pantheon of gods.

Those on the more progressive side of Christianity will argue that the codes established in Leviticus are outdated and meant for that particular group of people at that specific point in time. Although I can agree with this statement in most circumstances in the Old Testament — such as the prohibitions of eating shellfish and mixing fabrics — I don't think I can particularly agree when applying the same logic to Leviticus 18.

On the flipside, traditionalist Christians will say that Leviticus 18 is part of a code of morality that *does* apply to today's day and age. I will agree with that statement because it is indeed a code of morality that still applies. The problem is that traditionalist Christians tend to make this statement with the gay-bashing verse in mind, which I believe is inherently wrong.

I do not think God was wrong for forbidding incest, bestiality, or sacrificing your children in a fire for a Canaanite god. These things are wrong even by today's standard; however, I believe the true meaning of the *"lie with man"* section of verse 22 has been omitted and misinterpreted to fit an agenda that is highly anti-LGBT.

As we've discussed, the decrees in this chapter were specific in their purpose: setting the Jewish people apart from their slavers and neighbors. However, these decrees strongly alluded to ritualistic worship of the area's pagan gods. For example, the prohibition of incest was tediously laid out in every possible combination in verses 6-18. Why? Because the pantheon of Canaanite gods was infamously incestuous[4]:

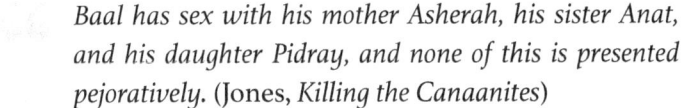

> *Baal has sex with his mother Asherah, his sister Anat,*
> *and his daughter Pidray, and none of this is presented*
> *pejoratively.* (Jones, *Killing the Canaanites*)

Additionally, in the *Egyptian Book of Dreams*, dreams of sexual relations with your mother or sister were considered good omens[5].

When you look at the surrounding verses, you will see that in verse 21, He also forbids the ritualistic sacrifice of children to the Canaanite god, Moloch [also written as Molak or Molek]. The Canaanites would often practice the barbaric sacrifice of their own children by burning them alive to appease the god Moloch in times of crisis and hardship[6].

In verse 23, we find the prohibition of bestiality and particular mention of women presenting themselves to animals for sexual intercourse. This is a familiar theme in Greek mythology when gods disguised as animals would rape young women, but let's take it closer to the Jewish nation's home. In the Canaanite epic poem, *The Baal Cycle*[7], we read,

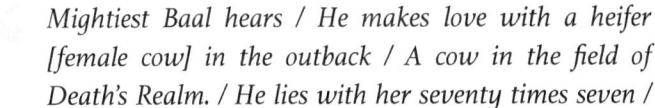

> *Mightiest Baal hears / He makes love with a heifer*
> *[female cow] in the outback / A cow in the field of*
> *Death's Realm. / He lies with her seventy times seven /*

> *Mounts eighty times eight / [She conceives] and bears a
> boy.* (Smith, *Ugaritic Narrative Poetry*, 148)

In *Killing the Canaanites*, Clay Jones also reveals that "in an
Egyptian dream book it was a bad omen for a woman to dream
about embracing her husband, but good things would happen if
she dreamed of intercourse with a baboon, wolf, or he-goat."

A clear pattern is observed with the listing of these prohibitions: they were condoned and encouraged by the different
pagan gods who would, at times, accept these practices as forms
of worship. So why would this alleged gay-bashing verse be
sandwiched in with the rest?

In the lands of Canaan, prostitution was often seen and used
as a popular form of worship. Ancient manuscripts often speak
of the goddess of sex, love, and fertility, Inanna (known as Ishtar
in Babylon), as having many temples strewn across the land of
Canaan. These temples' prized prostitutes were often homosexuals, transgender people, and *lewd* women used in sexual/or-
giastic rituals and religious festivals[8].

> *Even Uruk, the dwelling of Anu and Ishtar, city of pros-
> titutes, courtesans, and call-girls... they rouse Eanna,
> the party-boys and festival people who changed
> masculinity to femininity to make the people of Ishtar
> revere her.* (Dalley 1989, pg 305)

Understanding Canaanite culture is paramount in compre-
hending the sense behind the laws of Leviticus 18. Once we do,
we can make a logical conclusion – verse 22 is definitively
speaking of pagan ritualistic worship through homosexual prostitution *not* of homosexuality itself.

It is an unsound doctrine to be selective of texts while
ignoring their context. In a chapter relating to the worship of

pagan gods, isolating a section that pertains to homosexual relations as a standalone moral prohibition is self-serving to an
agenda that promotes hate and alienation of a people group
whose orientation is an intrinsic part of who they are.

 *Thou shalt not lie with mankind, as with womankind:
it is **abomination**.* (Leviticus 18:22, ASV)

Now let's look at this verse from another Christian perspective, specifically revolving around the word abomination. Let's
say our previous argument doesn't hold, and verse 22 can stand
by itself as a moral code — as written. That would mean that
God finds same-sex relations an abomination, right? Yes, that is,
if the word, abomination as originally written has the same
meaning as we define it today.

The word abomination is defined as a *vile, shameful, or
detestable action, condition, habit,* etc[9]. Casual readers of the Bible
tend to grab onto this translation as law and never fail to point to
it when speaking about loving the sinner but hating the sin of
homosexuality.

In all honesty, at first, I hesitated writing this section of the
book precisely because of this verse. I was overwhelmed by it,
considering my lack of degrees in theology or linguistics. I felt
like I didn't have enough knowledge to know how even to
explain the Biblical reasoning behind the choice of this word.

One day while I was listening to music and scrolling
through my phone in my living room, I saw a headline of a
young gay man from the UK who was assaulted to the point of
non-recognition, and almost immediately, I felt a massive tug at
my heart.

*You were called for this. Don't give up on the book. Remember
Peter and the animal sheet*, I heard almost as if a whisper. Sometimes, God has weird ways of speaking to me, but my favorites

are those small, barely comprehensible whispers. I was extremely confused.

Animal sheets? What?! I thought to myself, and then it hit me. I knew exactly what that message was about. So I pulled up Acts 10:9-15 for a refresher:

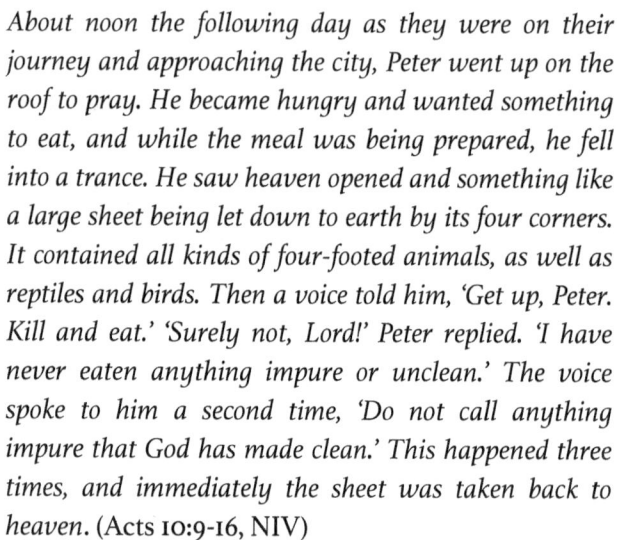

> *About noon the following day as they were on their journey and approaching the city, Peter went up on the roof to pray. He became hungry and wanted something to eat, and while the meal was being prepared, he fell into a trance. He saw heaven opened and something like a large sheet being let down to earth by its four corners. It contained all kinds of four-footed animals, as well as reptiles and birds. Then a voice told him, 'Get up, Peter. Kill and eat.' 'Surely not, Lord!' Peter replied. 'I have never eaten anything impure or unclean.' The voice spoke to him a second time, 'Do not call anything impure that God has made clean.' This happened three times, and immediately the sheet was taken back to heaven.* (Acts 10:9-16, NIV)

As with most of these theological analyses, I will never leave you hanging. In short, the Jewish culture believes certain animals to be unclean and unholy for consumption. Likewise, Jewish traditions decreed a clear distinction between Jew and Gentile (non-Jewish person) and that God favored the Jews above all nations as His chosen people. The importance of this verse in the New Testament shows a shift in God's treatment of humans from a period of law, governed by the Mosaic laws of the Old Testament, to a period of grace, governed by the words of Jesus.

When the voice said to Peter, *do not call anything impure that God has made clean*, it showed Peter that the customs once governed by the Old Laws no longer applied after the sacrifice of Jesus. Minutes later, servants of a Roman centurion showed up at his doorstep, requesting that Peter come quickly as an angel had told their Roman master that Peter had a message to impart. Usually, a Jewish person would never waste their time giving divine assistance or guidance to a Gentile [non-Jew], but as God instructed in the vision, *do not call him impure if I have made him clean*. The next day, Peter accompanied them to the Roman centurions' house and the entire household accepted the faith of Jesus.

Okay... So what does this have anything to do with the word abomination? I had been wrestling with this for weeks, and I felt like this was the answer I needed somehow. Still, I didn't recognize the answer until I started looking into it.

The Hebrew word from which the translation of abomination originates is pronounced *teovah*, found on multiple occasions in the Bible. This article by William Crawley explains it well[10],

> *There is widespread agreement among Hebrew scholars that the word "teovah" as used in Leviticus is not, in fact, a moral term; instead, it is a cultic term which indicates "ritual uncleanness". Any action that is said to be "teovah" is an action which requires a person to engage in ritual purification before they may come to worship. Sometimes, the term "teovah" can be used in the Bible to refer simply to sinful behaviour in general, but in the case of the text in question, scholars agree that ritual uncleanness is implied.* (Crawley, June 2008)

Mr. Crawley might be on to something! Here are a few other instances of the word *teovah* being used in the Bible:

> *Do not eat any detestable [teovah] thing. These are the animals you may eat: the ox, the sheep, [...] they are ceremonially unclean [teovah] for you. The pig is also unclean; although it has a divided hoof, it does not chew the cud. You are not to eat their meat or touch their carcasses.* (Deuteronomy 14:3-8, NIV)

> *...then her first husband, who divorced her, is not allowed to marry her again after she has been defiled [by her second marriage after the second husband dies]. That would be detestable [teovah] in the eyes of the Lord. Do not bring sin upon the land the Lord your God is giving you as an inheritance."* (Deuteronomy 24:4, NIV)

> *[...] In you one man commits a detestable [toevah] offense with his neighbor's wife, another shamefully defiles his daughter-in-law, and another violates his sister, his own father's daughter. [...]* (Ezekiel 22:11, NIV)

> *Stop bringing meaningless offerings! Your incense is detestable [teovah] to me. New Moons, Sabbaths and convocations— I cannot bear your worthless assemblies.* (Isaiah 1:13, NIV)

As you can see, the instances of the word *teovah* range from food, divorce, adultery, empty offerings, and more. Interestingly enough, many translations have corrected the Leviticus 18:22 verse to read *detestable* instead of an *abomination*. Yet older translations would pick and choose when to use this heavier word, leaving it out for instances of adultery and divorce, but making sure to include it when allegedly addressing homosexuality.

Truly, a prime example of double standards and a possible alternative agenda.

To conclude my thoughts on Leviticus 18, it is difficult to escape the logic when you look at the contextual clues all around it. Even if you ignore the strong contextual evidence and focus solely on the word *abomination*, you will still find a weak argument of a "*depravity*" placed on an equal level as certain foods, divorce, or cheating. All actions that simply left someone ritually unclean and required purification before worshiping.

If a literal translation is accepted, we find more questions than absolute certainty – based on this verse, are lesbians free to act on their passions? Are female same-sex relations not considered an abomination, but male same-sex relations are?

Furthermore, if the story of the animal sheet serves as a moral compass of what is clean vs. unclean, then maybe we should abandon our desire to diminish people we think to be impure and start looking at them through God's eyes of grace. After all, it was an order made to Peter three consecutive times, "*Do not call anything impure that God has made clean.*"

This same message applies to you. Don't let those who call you impure because of who you love serve as a stumbling block in your journey. God has called you and made you clean through salvation in Christ.

BITE SIZED SUMMARY
Leviticus 18:22

THE CHURCH'S CRUMBS: Verse 22 is clear that same-sex relations are considered an abomination in God's eyes — you can't get any clearer!

SPILLING THE TEA: The entirety of Leviticus 18 lays out prohibitions of practices that were often used in ritual or religious traditions in the lands of Egypt and Canaan. When considering the culture of the Canaanites and the Egyptians, these prohibitions distinctly refer to acts that the pagan gods of both groups condoned.

Verse 22, in specific, may refer to the famous temple prostitutes of the Canaanite goddess Innana/Ishtar, whose prized *party-boys* were highly regarded temple prostitutes. These temples were famous throughout all of Canaan.

Another weak argument I've recently read tries to argue that "if these things are only a sin in the context of ritual worship, then does that make incest, bestiality, or sacrificing children, okay outside of the context of worship?"

This argument seems to be an "aha, got you!" moment for many Christians, and quite frankly, it is incredibly ridiculous. On the topic of child sacrifice, *thou shalt not kill*, rings some major bells. In terms of bestiality, we find multiple instances of prohibition throughout the Bible (i.e. Exodus 22:19,

Deuteronomy 27:12). We also see numerous accounts of prohibitions of incest (i.e Ezekiel 22:11, Deuteronomy 27:20, 22-23). All this considered, outside of Leviticus 18 and 20, we see nothing else allegedly referring to homosexuality in the Old Testament. We'll be analyzing the New Testament shortly.

Leviticus 20:13

If a man has sexual relations with a man as one does with a woman, both of them have done what is detestable. They are to be put to death; their blood will be on their own heads. (Leviticus 20:13)

Ouch, harsh, isn't it? Leviticus 20:13 is nothing more than an accompanying verse to that of 18:22. In this chapter many of the laws listed out in chapter 18 and 19 are restated with their intended "lawful" consequences. It is illogical to isolate this single verse as a standalone argument against homosexuality after it, very clearly, reviews the previous couple of chapters of stated prohibitions with the addition of their penalties.

If you are familiar with how laws are written, on many occasions the code of law will state what is and isn't prohibited and additional documentation will follow up with what the penalties will be for those who break said laws. We find this similarity within these three chapters, and in them, the same concepts of our last section still apply. Laws require consequences if broken. If chapters 18 and 19 lay out these laws, it is only natural that a chapter on consequences for breaking the laws would follow soon after.

If anyone were to take this verse as a standalone argument against homosexuality, they definitely wouldn't be able to negate the rest of the verses that: put someone's cheating husband/wife to death along with their lover (verse 10), executes someone who curses their parents (verse 9), or completely cuts off from society those who have sex with women on their periods (verse 6 & 18).

BITE SIZED SUMMARY
Leviticus 20:13

THE CHURCH'S CRUMBS: Homosexuality is such a grave sin that its punishment is listed as death. Clearly, something must be seriously wrong with it for the Bible to warrant an execution!

SPILLING THE TEA: You can't cherry-pick verses in the Bible and expect people to take it as law. As we've seen, there's context to this verse in the previous chapters.

Likewise, if you *are* going to cherry-pick the verse on alleged homosexuality, then you should be okay with carrying out the rest of the punishments too. Hypothetically, if you're truly a proponent of these verses, then you would agree that a strip club full of married men should also have a crazed shooter kill them for simply for being there [our community has, when 49 innocent people were shot down at the Orlando Pulse gay nightclub]. (Verse 10)

Or maybe once we find out which men have sex with women on their periods, we should be allowed to beat them to non-recognition on the streets [like many gay people have, simply for walking down the sidewalk and looking a certain way]. (Verse 18)

Maybe we should implement a law that allows Child Protective Services to immediately take a child from their family if they speak badly about their parents on any level [like a Texas law's attempt of accusing the parents of transgender children of child abuse]. (Verse 9)

You cannot make one Bible verse law, while diminishing the validity of the others surrounding it. All of these terrible events that have occurred within the LGBT+ community are a *direct* result of a society that chose ignorance of a holy scripture over true understanding.

Hi, my name is Paul.

Before we dive into the New Testament texts, we need a little background on its author. All the gay bashing texts that are found in the New Testament were thought to be written by the apostle Paul. Who is this Paul guy, and why was he so important? Well for one, his name was originally Saul.

Saul was born a Jew in the city of Tarsus, a capital of the Roman province of Cilicia, modern-day Turkey. We know Saul was of Jewish background because of his mention of circumcision, a practice that was a cornerstone for identifying Jewish males.

Circumcision was a sense of pride for Jewish men. If you've dug into Biblical history, being circumcised was a hot ticket item of debate for the early church. The question of whether or not you would be saved if you were "*uncut*" was something that was hotly debated in the ancient church, but that's a topic for another racy book.

We see Paul's borderline boasting of his circumcision in his letter to the Philippians while trying to convince them that being "*circumcised of the Spirit*" was more important than in the flesh.

> *for we are the circumcision, who worship by the Spirit of God, and glory in Christ Jesus, and have no confidence in the flesh: though I myself might have confidence even in the flesh: if any other man thinketh to have confidence in the flesh, I yet more: circumcised the eighth day, of the stock of Israel, of the tribe of Benjamin, a Hebrew of Hebrews; as touching the law, a Pharisee.* (Philippians 3:3-5, ASV)

Saul was a particularly great candidate for God's use. Not only did he hold Jewish principles, but he was also lucky enough to have been born a Roman citizen – a perk that was hard to come by with benefits that surpassed most luxuries in the ancient world. Although Roman citizenship could be bought at the time, it was generally a perk reserved only for the rich as the process was pricey.

Being born into Roman citizenship offered Saul freedom to travel the known world under the protection of Roman law. This perk saved Saul countless times from persecution as he preached the Gospel. It once even landed him an appearance before the Roman emperor Nero. As a Jew and educated Roman citizen, Saul knew both Aramaic (language of the Jewish people), the widely known Greek, and we can assume some Latin from his Roman citizenship. Still, before Saul was considered a man of God, he was seen as the vilest villain to all Christians, apart from Emperor Nero and the devil himself.

You see, Paul was a devout Jew who would eventually travel to Jerusalem and attach himself to the Jewish High Priest as his hired thug. It was Saul's mission to scope out Christians and persecute them, and he was good at it. Though his exact atrocities were never listed in detail, he did admit to dragging men and women from their Christian gatherings to prisons and beating them. If what happened to them was similar to what the

Jewish leaders did to the newly transformed Paul, it wasn't pretty[11].

Saul's conversion to Christianity, which warranted a change in name to Paul, came about on his journey to Damascus on a mission of persecution. He had been ordered by the chief priests to go to Damascus, round up any Christians, and bring them back as prisoners to Jerusalem. On the way to Damascus, Saul's journey was interrupted by a vision – a flash of light came from the heavens and a voice said, "Saul, Saul, why do you persecute me[12]?" Others in his traveling party claim to have heard the voice but did not see anyone; Saul, on the other hand, saw a man[13]. When he questioned who this man was, the man responded that he was the resurrected Jesus.

It was there that Jesus gave him a new mission, to receive further instructions in Damascus about how he would be used to change the world. From that day on, Saul the persecutor became Paul the apostle, heavily responsible for spreading the Gospel across the then-known world.

1 Corinthians 6:9-10

In 1 Corinthians 6:9-10, the apostle Paul writes to the believers in Corinth and lays out some examples of those who would not inherit the Kingdom of God. Within the verses it is *believed* he makes mention of homosexuality, but even in these translations we see a variety of different interpretations of the same section.

As we analyze these different translations, I'll place the specific wording relating to what has been construed as homosexuality in bold and add dates in which each translation was published.

The Wycliffe Bible is considered the first handwritten translation of the Bible into English, dated back to 1382. We'll start off with this version.

> *Whether ye know not, that wicked men shall not wield the kingdom of God? Do not ye err; neither lechers, neither men that serve maumets [neither men serving to idols], neither adulterers, neither **lechers against kind, neither they that do lechery with men**, neither thieves, neither avaricious men [neither covetous men, or niggards (meaning stingy or ungenerous)], neither men full of drunkenness, neither cursers, neither raveners, shall wield the kingdom of God. And ye were sometime these things [And these things ye were sometime]; but ye be washed, but ye be hallowed, but ye be justified in the name of our Lord Jesus Christ, and in the Spirit of our God.* (1 Corinthians 6:9-13, Wycliffe Bible, 1382)

If you're a modern human like me, you probably have no clue what *lechers* or *lechery* mean, so here are a few definitions:

- Lechery is a noun applied to a person's feelings that are lustful or sexual in an extreme or unnatural way. A person's lechery may lead to wrong and unlawful physical acts or attacks on others (Vocabulary.com)
- Unrestrained or excessive indulgence of sexual desire. (Dictionary.com)
- Inordinate [exceeding reasonable limits] indulgence in sexual activity (Merriam-Webster Dictionary)
- Excessive or offensive sexual desire; lustfulness. (Oxford Languages)

So, lechery in this sense of the meaning is an over-exaggerated lust, often bordering the lines of offense or attack on another – an abnormal over-the-top sexual desire that we could even relate to sex addiction and assault. Keep this in mind as we explore further.

The William Tyndale version of the Bible is considered the first printed English version of the Bible[14] back in the 1500s. Keep in mind these versions written in old English use printing techniques that often-substituted certain letters for others to make it easier for print, so you'll find it to be spelled a bit differently than what we are used to.

> *Do ye not remember how that the vnrighteous shall not inheret the kyngdome of God? Be not deceaved. For nether fornicators nether worshyppers of ymages nether whormongers nether **weaklinges** nether **abusars of them selves with the mankynde** nether theves nether the coveteous nether dronkardes nether cursed speakers nether pillers shall inheret the kyngdome of God. And soche ware ye verely: but ye are wesshed: ye are sanctified: ye are iustified by the name of the Lorde Iesus and by the sprete of oure God.* (1 Corinthians 6:9-11, Tyndale Bible, 1534)

As you can see, in the first English versions of the Bible, the placeholder that has often been replaced with some form of the word *homosexual* was originally translated as *lecher* and *lechers against kind* (someone with over-exaggerated and unrestrained sexual desire against others and against the same sex).

The Tyndale Bible then changes *lechers* to *weakling*, with a completely different definition and weight. Now here is how that phrase has changed in English translations used today:

[...]nor **effeminate**, nor **abusers of themselves with mankind,**

1 Corinthians 6:9 (King James Version, 1604)

[...] nor *effeminate*, nor *abusers of themselves with men*, (American Standard Version, 1901)

[...] nor *men who have sex with men* (New International Version, 1973, Updated 2011)

[...] nor *effeminate*, nor *homosexuals*, (New American Standard Bible, 1995)

[...] nor *homosexuals*, (New American Standard Bible Revised Version, considered to be the "most accurate," 1970 updated in 2020)

From *lechers* and *abusers of mankind* to a direct *men who have sex with men* and *homosexuals* seems like quite a huge jump in meaning. If you remember in our earlier chapters, Martin Luther was responsible for the first printed, less-complex, translation of the Bible from the ancient languages into common German. His translation can be considered the first easy-to-digest translation in a contemporary language. Let's take a look.

 Wisset ihr nicht, daß die Ungerechten das Reich Gottes nicht ererben werden? Lasset euch nicht verführen! Weder die Hurer noch die Abgöttischen noch die Ehebrecher noch die **Weichlinge** *noch die* **Knabenschänder [...]** (1 Corinthians 6:9, Luther Bible, 1534)

For those of you who do not read German, *Weichlinge* is the equivalent of *weakling*, while *Knabenschänder* is the literal equivalent of *boy molester*. While the word for soft or weakling has remained consistent to a definition pointing to laziness or degeneracy, how can a word defined as boy molester, an abuser, make the enormous jump to homosexual? As we move up the telephone game's line of communication, closer to the original manuscript, we uncover the potential disconnect of scholarly interpreters.

As we've learned, the New Testament was mostly written in koine Greek. 1 Corinthians was a letter written by the apostle Paul to the small community of believers in Corinth, a city in south-central Greece. In his letter, he addresses the community's questions and concerns over the issues experienced among them. Understanding who his target audience was, he writes back in a way they would understand – in koine Greek.

To contextualize what is going on in this chapter, from the beginning, Paul scolds the Corinthian believers for the number of injustices occurring within their community. These injustices are so rampant, believers are taking each other to the courts to be judged by (who Paul refers to as) the ungodly [pagans, unrighteous, etc], instead of handling justice among themselves. Furthermore, he makes an audacious statement that it is better to be the victim of an injustice than to be a community of believers committing the crimes themselves!

 The very fact that you have lawsuits among you means you have been completely defeated already. Why not rather be wronged? Why not rather be cheated? Instead, you yourselves cheat and do wrong, and you do this to your brothers and sisters. Or do you not know that wrongdoers will not inherit the kingdom of God? (1 Corinthians 6:7-9, NIV)

He then goes on to list our verses in question, stating a myriad of behaviors that caused injustice to occur among these believers; from drunkenness to prostitution, and from hoarding wealth to predatory behaviors, all of which cause much of the discord and lawsuits among the believers of Corinth – so where does homosexuality fit into this?

Here is how that verse reads in the original manuscript, the first line in Greek, the second line as the phonetic pronunciation, the third line with the translation, and our words in question are in bold:

μη
(mé)
Do not

πλανάσθε
(planaó)
be misled

ούτε
(oute)
neither

πόρνοι
(pornos)
Prostitute
from pernaō
to sell off

ούτε
(oute)
neither

εἰδωλολάτραι
(eidólolatrés)
image worshippers
idolaters

οὔτε
(oute)
neither

μοιχοί
(moichos)
adulterers

οὔτε
(oute)
neither

μαλακοί
(Malakos)
soft

οὔτε
(oute)
neither

αρσενοκοίται
(arsenokoites)
Contested word, see below
alleged to be homosexual or man who sleeps with man.

The two words that have caused an outcry and much debate in the theologian community are that of *malakos* and *arsenokoites*. People don't seem to agree on its intended meaning. Let's start with the one that has more factual evidence to back it up: *malakos.*

As we dive in, I must make clear that I struggled to find a Greek lexicon (ancient language dictionary) resource that did not have some sort of religious influence. I attempted to look for a resource that was purely academic because, with it, I knew I would read definitions free of the influence of centuries of religious dogmas (beliefs, teachings, convictions, etc) and could also provide additional resources of other contemporary literature of the time for cross-referencing the use of the same word.

Using a more secular-based lexicon vs. a religious one gives us better view of how the word may have been used in context of the writing of that time without solely basing our findings on Biblical scripture. In the end, I found a webpage of the Harvard University Classics Department that led me to the Thesaurus Linguae Graecae (TLG)® along with other ancient text dictionaries[15].

Malakos

Malakos when translated literally, simply means soft. Out of curiosity, I asked my Greek friend, Dimitris, of its meaning in case the word had survived these thousands of years into modern day Greek. Much to my surprise and anticlimactically enough, he said *malakos* simply meant soft. *Groundbreaking, isn't it?*

According to him, it was used both as an adjective for something such as clothing, as well as to mean an overly sensitive person. It seemed to check out! Here are some other references in the original ancient Greek translation of the Bible where *malakos* was used:

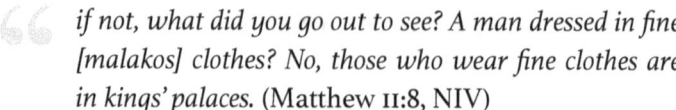

> *if not, what did you go out to see? A man dressed in fine [malakos] clothes? No, those who wear fine clothes are in kings' palaces.* (Matthew 11:8, NIV)

The same story, as told by Luke, contains the same verbiage,

> *If not, what did you go out to see? A man dressed in fine [malakos] clothes? No, those who wear expensive clothes and indulge in luxury are in palaces.* (Luke 7:25, NIV)

In the TLG® we are reminded how Greek words can have a variety of different meanings based on context. Although soft, gentle, and kind are among the definitions of *malakos*, Paul has a more aggressive and scolding tone towards the believers in Corinth. Because of this, we should look at the definitions with a more negative connotation.

1. *Soft*

Examples of *malakos* here is used in the Greek text of *Thucydides*, referring to a military general that was not yet admiral. Perhaps *too soft* to be admiral[16]. In Plato's *Republic* the same word is used to describe those who have been raised to be spoiled, "*too soft* to stand against pleasure and pain[17]"

2. *Faint-hearted; cowardly*

Also in *Thucydides*, *malakos* is used to mean coward when encouraging wise men to deliver their minds freely in speaking against the Peloponnesian war; not to fear being seen as *cowards* for doing so[18].

3. *Morally weak; lacking in self-control*

In Aristotle's *Nicomachean Ethics*, the word *malakos* is used in the context of a type of person who is self-indulgent and lacks control for said indulgences. Indulgences here relate to luxuries and pleasures of life rather than strictly a sexual meaning. In the text, Aristotle writes that the avoidance of pain and suffering for self-indulgence brings about a *softness* to a man[19].

4. Of music: soft and effeminate

In Plato's, *Republic*, a discussion on the different modes [styles] of music identifies certain styles of the Iodian and Lydian modes of Greek music to be *malakos*. Through context, it seems these musical styles were known to evoke a feeling of *laziness and effeminacy*. Within the discussion, the music is said to be even useless to women, a misogynistic point we'll touch on soon. The Greeks in this discussion were contesting what we know today as music's ability to affect our emotions[20] and make us feel lazy.

In all of these definitions, we do not see homosexuality in any form. Even the word *effeminate*, as we see in many modern-day English translations, is a point of contention. Effeminacy to the Greeks was not as we see it today; the term had a much broader definition than simply looking like or having the mannerisms of women.

To the very misogynistic culture of the Ancient Greeks, to be a woman was to be weak. They were seen, in many ways, as second-class citizens. To be called effeminate, was an insult different than how we may perceive it today. Effeminacy was not strictly measured by the physical perception of a man. In fact, cross-dressing was a cultural norm at the time; from religious ceremonies to the performing arts, men would often dress like women. Even in stories of great masculine heroes, like Achilles, we see him dressed as a woman to hide from being drafted into a senseless war.

Effeminacy to the ancient Greeks was primarily measured by the mental and emotional traits of a person. Excessive kindness, gentleness, shyness, gullibility, self-indulgence, clumsiness, laziness, submissiveness, lack of courage, among other negative traits they would often attribute to women, would make a man effeminate in a Greek man's eyes. These grave insults that touch on a man's character often warranted a grave reaction.

In Plutarch's, *Amatorius*, a strange story is told when the tyrant Periander mocks his boy lover in front of a group of people. Periander publicly asks his lover if he was pregnant yet, highly offending his *eromenos* [boy lover, to be discussed soon] and causes the boy to kill Periander in revenge. Comparison to a woman was an attack of character not to be taken lightly.

Understanding the root origin of this word and its cultural context gives new light to Paul's original letter to the Corinthians. Here we can come to understand that his version of *malakos* most likely meant something along the lines of self-indulgent or degeneracy when taking its context into consideration — both representing negative qualities seen by the ancient Greeks as *womanly*.

Arsenokoites

Things get a bit more complicated when talking about the latter word in the verse, *arsenokoites*. This word was actually made up by Paul, which before him, had never been seen in any ancient Greek literary works. Theologians believe he coined this term based on his knowledge of the Greek version of the Old Testament, specifically Leviticus 18, that would have been available to him[21].

Within this newly coined term are the words *arsen* meaning male and *koite* meaning "to bed," specifically the marriage bed, or sexual intercourse. Combined, it would be fair to assume that he means to take a man to your marriage bed, or to have sexual intercourse with the man. Things get messy here in terms of interpretation.

On one hand, if theologians are right in that Paul is specifically making mention of Leviticus 18, we have already covered that the verse is in context of ritualistic worship through the same-sex prostitutes of the temples of Ishtar. Although Ishtar was not a prominent goddess of ancient Greece or Rome, deities such as Aphrodite and Venus of the Greek and Roman pantheons, respectively, facilitated similar practices in their temples[22]. Our argument would still stand strong in pointing to homosexual prostitution as commonly used in ritualistic worship.

On the other hand, if the word was a bit more literal in terms of taking a man to your marriage bed, it is quite possible we're talking about pederasty. Pederasty was an extremely common practice in Classical Greece and, in certain instances, in Rome where an older man, *erastes*, usually in his 20s or older (whether married, single, straight, or a homosexual) would take on a boy lover, *eromenos*, usually in his teens. For many in these cultures, this was considered a rite of passage from boyhood to manhood.

In Greece, these sexual relationships were often seen as an apprenticeship where, aside from sexual intercourse, the *eromenos* boy would often benefit from a mentorship from the *erastes* man to further his role in society. Take it back a few generations, into the time of the Old Testament, and you would find this was especially true in Sparta where this kind of pederastic relationship was a mandatory part of a young Spartan's education[23]. This practice lived on through the centuries.

Rome was more selective with pederasty. As an empire priding itself in superiority over those it conquered, Romans saw pederasty in a light of dominance and power. It was taboo for Romans to be on the receiving, more submissive end of such a relationship (the "*bottom*"), thus Roman men would often assert the dominant role (the "*top*") while slaves and servants of non-Roman descent would fulfill the submissive role without much benefit in return.

Homosexuality, although common in Greece, may not have been as common in Rome because of its cultural taboo – a debacle better summarized around the issue of who was *top* and who was *bottom*. We'll discuss this culture of Roman imperialism in the next sections.

In both circumstances, an imbalance of power is clearly observed between those in a position of power vs. those who must submit to that power. This imbalance is most apparent in the difference in age. Interestingly enough, Paul's choice of words through use of the term *arsen* comes into question, both in this verse and in his letter to the Romans.

The words *arsen/arren* generally related to males without discrimination of age, while an alternative term of *aner* pertained primarily to adult men. In J.E. Miller's *Response: Pederasty and Romans 1:27: A Response to Mark Smith*, Miller makes the connection between Paul's choice of words and his Jewish background, while pointing out that homosexuality was already a taboo subject in Roman culture[24]:

 Early Jewish sources frequently attacked homosexuality, and when they did so they specifically specified it as pederasty. Important for understanding [...] is the frequent use of arsen/arren (male, not age specific) and the rarity of the term aner (man/adult male) in these Jewish attacks on pederasty. The use of non-age specific term is sometimes a code-word for the adolescent boy, and in other cases it is used for both ages to emphasize the sameness of the two where a gentile author would emphasize the age difference. [...] First, Paul is attacking an accepted Gentile practice. Homosexuality between males was not an accepted activity, but pederasty was.

> *Second, in light of Jewish polemic against Gentile prac-*
> *tices, by using the term arsen Paul implies that at least*
> *one of the males involved is not an aner [adult male].*
> (Miller, pg 863)

Were the believers of the Greek Corinthian community having pederastic issues? It is highly probable. With Roman influence, it was even more likely that these relationships reflected those of abusive power over same-sex servants and slaves that likely had little say in the matter.

If we look at earlier English translations of the bible, which mention boy molesters, abusers of mankind, and the like, we start seeing a much clearer picture of the game of telephone that perhaps was misinterpreted. It becomes clear that Paul was addressing issues of pederasty and abuse within the community of believers.

Likewise, we should remember that one of the definitions of the *koite* portion of *arsenokoites* means a bed or, in most cases, a marriage bed. It is equally as valid to consider that married men within the Corinthian community were taking their boy slaves and servants as lovers, equating to both a sin of abuse *and* adultery.

BITE SIZED SUMMARY
1 Corinthians 6: 9-10

THE CHURCH'S CRUMBS: Paul clearly states that the effeminate and men who have sex with men (homosexuals in some translations) are not going to inherit the kingdom of God.

SPILLING THE TEA: Effeminacy, as we see it today, was not the same interpretation from the perspective of the ancient Greeks and Romans of Corinth. What made a man effeminate may have weighed more heavily on a man's character and habits, as well as the hypermasculine ideal of whether you took an active or passive role in sex, than it did on physical appearance and mannerisms.

As for the latter part of the verse, it is hermeneutically unsound to take a completely new word coined by the author and apply it to an interpretation without taking into consideration the cultural norms of the region and time period. In this particular instance, it is highly likely that the community of believers in Corinth were having issues of grave pederasty where older men were taking advantage of young men and boys as lovers, sex slaves, and the like, even while married.

Romans 1: 26-27

Alright, so we've covered pederasty in 1 Corinthians, but surely in Romans the Bible is clear on homosexuality, right? Let's look at a few different translations:

> *For this cause God gave them up unto vile passions: for their **women changed the natural use into that which is against nature:** and likewise also the **men, leaving the natural use of the woman, burned in their lust one toward another, men with men working unseemliness,** and receiving in themselves that recompense of their error which was due.* (Romans 1:26- 27, ASV)

> *Because of this, God gave them over to shameful lusts. Even their **women exchanged natural sexual relations for unnatural ones.** In the same way the **men also abandoned natural relations with women and were inflamed with lust for one another. Men committed shameful acts with other men,** and received in themselves the due penalty for their error.* (Romans 1:26-27, NIV)

It seems straightforward, right? At least, that is what the church will claim without any further thought in the matter. Paul seemingly lays out that same-sex relations are unnatural and vile in the eyes of God. As with many other gay-bashing verses, it is amazing how those who have been indoctrinated in this subject always fail to contextualize the verses they read. To understand the next point I'm going to make, let's suppose you receive this note from me:

Hey, you!
The best coxinhas [co-sheen-yas] will be found at Amor em Pedaços.
Be sure to only go during the week, because it will be packed on
weekends. Highly recommend!

Do you have any clue of what I'm talking about? If you're Brazilian or are familiar with Brazilian culture, you will know that *coxinhas* are a popular fried salted dough stuffed with chicken that are incredibly flavorful. Still, even if you are Brazilian, you may not know what *Amor em Pedaços* is unless you live in or have visited Orlando and recognize that it is a popular Brazilian bakery in the area.

Perhaps if you were neither Brazilian nor familiar with the area, you could have used context clues to determine that I was recommending some type of food from a restaurant, but unless you are *both* part of the Brazilian culture (or familiar with it) and live in/have visited Orlando, Florida, you will likely not understand the exact meaning of my message.

We can make the same connection to Paul's letter to the Romans. To read Paul's letter, you have to place yourself in the shoes of the letter's intended recipients – the first century Romans. During the first century, the Roman empire was intrinsically a pagan society. The capital of Rome was full of temples dedicated to the dozens of gods within the Greco-Roman pantheon: Jupiter, Neptune, Venus, and many other minor deities. Within this society stemmed hundreds of cults, each with varying customs and ritualistic practices.

Venus, in particular, was held in high regard by Romans, exemplified by the various prominent temples built in her honor, such as the temple of *Venus Genetrix* and *Venus Victrix*[25]. As the goddess of love, fertility, and prostitution, Venus' sacred and promiscuous temple prostitution was widespread and commonplace. In fact, it was so popular that the conservative Roman aristocracy eventually attempted to promote and dedicate a temple to *Venus Verticordia*, "Turner of Hearts," in an attempt to shift ideals from those of lust to chastity[26].

Interestingly enough, a fifth-century account of a Roman provincial by the name of Macrobius gives us an account of how the goddess was seen in the eyes of the Romans[27],

> *Moreover, there is in Cyprus a bearded statue of the goddess with female clothing but with male attributes, so that it would seem that the deity is both male and female. Aristophanes also calls her 'Aphroditus'; and in Laevinus the descriptive adjective is in the masculine gender, when he says: 'Therefore worshipping Venus the giver of life, whether the deity is female or male—even as is the life-giving deity that shines by night.' Philochorus, too, in his Atthis says that Venus is the moon and that men offer sacrifice to the moon dressed as women, and women dressed as men, because the moon is thought to be both male and female.* (Macrobius, *The Saturnalia, c.a. 431 AD*)

Along with the cult of Venus, another popular cult was that of *Cybele*, also known as the *Magna Mater* (Great Mother), a fertility deity imported from the region of Phrygia (Western Turkey.) This particular cult was highly controversial in Roman society due to its graphic ritualistic celebrations. The festival held in honor of Cybele, known as the *Megalesia*, involved various processions of great debauchery and outrageous behaviors that ruled the streets of Rome.

The depravity was often so outrageous that the conservative elites of Roman society would usually avoid them, naming the festival as a festival for *plebeians,* or commoners[28]. The festival culminated into what was known as the rites of the *Day of Blood*[29], which were ceremonies that initiated Cybele's androgynous eunuch priests into the priesthood.

Men would engage in orgiastic rituals and dances, eventually ending in a bloody act of self-mutilation and self-castration as a surrender of their fertility to the goddess of fertility herself. These priests, known as the *Galli*, would have open sex and later, quite literally, surrender their "manhood" in the worship of the Great Mother.

These rituals were often public and gruesomely graphic, yet still, a commonly observed part of Roman life. Lynn E. Roller, a Professor of Classics at the University of California Davis, further clarifies the significance[30] of this cult in Roman society,

 The Magna Mater lies within the group of officially recognized state cults, yet outside the bounds of decent behavior, thereby, offering the chance of an illicit, and potentially titillating, experience. The male participant in the cult could toy with transvestitism, bisexuality, and emotional release, all within one of Rome's most hallowed shrines. Thus the appeal of the cult appears to lie in the narrator's need to come to terms with both sides of his nature, the lawful and the lascivious. (L.E. Roller, 1999)

We see another popular cult in Roman Society with the cult

of Isis. Imported from Roman-controlled Egypt, the Egyptian deity was often represented as a human female, accompanied by Horus, portrayed as half-falcon/half-man. Other gods of the Egyptian pantheon were celebrated alongside her, such as the god Anubis (dog/jackal-headed) and other animal/human hybrid deities. This cult was particularly prevalent among the women and lower class of Rome to such an extent that the Roman elite feared it would unite the lower classes and issued decrees to destroy their temples at one point in history[31].

The cult of Isis had a particularly flamboyant celebration in March, where a procession of beautifully decorated carts, finely dressed performers wearing costumes of the half-human-half-animal deities, and sacred objects would be paraded through the streets to honor Isis. The purpose of these processions was to plead the goddess for a safe harbor for the city's ships[32].

So, what do any of these popular cults have to do with Paul and his letter to the Romans? Once you have an insight into the customs of these cults, you realize that this was everyday life for the Roman citizens. Romans were used to seeing these bizarre religious spectacles, processions, and celebrations on a reoccurring basis.

If you read Romans 1:18-27, you can *now* interpret it through this perspective of Roman life. Let's read the entire message Paul wrote preceding verses 26 and 27:

> *The wrath of God is being revealed from heaven against all the godlessness and wickedness of people, who suppress the truth by their wickedness, since what may be known about God is plain to them, because God has made it plain to them. For since the creation of the world God's invisible qualities—his eternal power and divine nature—have been clearly seen, being understood from what has been made, so that people are*

*without excuse. For although they knew God, they neither glorified him as God nor gave thanks to him, but their thinking became futile and their foolish hearts were darkened. Although they claimed to be wise, they became fools and **exchanged the glory of the immortal God for images made to look like a mortal human being and birds and animals and reptiles. <u>Therefore</u>** God gave them over in the sinful desires of their hearts to **sexual impurity for the degrading of their bodies with one another.** They exchanged the truth about God for a lie, and **worshiped and served created things rather than the Creator**—who is forever praised. Amen.* (Romans 1:18-25, NIV)

In these verses, Paul argues that God has always made Himself known to humans through His creation. Paul asserts that because we see the majesty of nature and all God has created, we then have knowledge of God. However, as he points out accusingly against the pagans, they have taken the essence of God "[...] and exchanged the glory of the immortal God for images made to look like a mortal human being and birds and animals and reptiles" (Romans 1:23).

To a Roman audience, the processions of the cult of Isis and its half-human and half-animal pantheon may have immediately come to mind. Paul says that God has surrendered them to the desires and depravities of their hearts *because* of this.

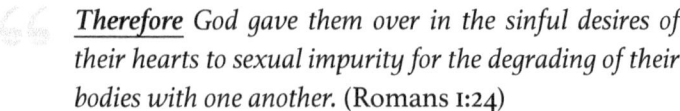

<u>Therefore</u> *God gave them over in the sinful desires of their hearts to sexual impurity for the degrading of their bodies with one another.* (Romans 1:24)

While speaking of this kind of idolatry, Paul then introduces the concepts we see in verses 26 and 27. Aside from Rome, these goddess cults were widespread throughout the Roman-controlled Mediterranean territories. There is a high probability that Paul had encountered or heard of these different cultic practices from other cities he had previously visited.

In Ephesus, where one community of believers lived, temples of Cybele as Ephesian Artemis and Venus were popular. It is incredibly plausible, and more than likely, that Paul's mention of men exchanging their "natural sexual relations for unnatural ones" directly connects to his criticism of the rituals performed in these cults; particularly, the gruesome and promiscuous rites of cult of Cybele/Magna Mater/Ephesian Artemis and Venus/Aphrodite. To the first-century Romans, Paul's letter immediately recalled the familiar images they experienced in the very streets of Rome: orgies, debauchery, and religious/ceremonial cross-dressing.

To further enforce this point of view, it's essential to understand that homosexual relations were *already* a societal taboo to the Romans. Romans prided themselves on a patriarchal culture of power and masculinity. They were conquerors of the then-known world and took pride in this "*penetration*" mentality. Today, we call that toxic masculinity. To Romans, men were expected to perform the active (*top*) role in sexual relations, and to be the submissive (*bottom/receiving*) role was attributed to women and slaves.

If you were a Roman accused of fulfilling the submissive role, enemies and friends often ridiculed you. Julius Caesar, for example, was ridiculed by his enemies and nicknamed the "Queen of Bithynia" after rumors spread that he submitted himself to the submissive role in an affair with Nicomedes, the King of Bithynia[33].

Ironically, pederasty was still acceptable if the submissive role was a non-Roman boy. It seems that younger boys were considered feminine in the eyes of Roman men and thus satisfactory in their sexual involvement until they began demonstrating more masculine features.

Why would Paul further call out as sin what had already been shunned by Roman society? It makes far more logical sense that in a chapter speaking directly of idolatry, as Paul makes mention of images that would be memorable to the Romans' experience of cultic traditions, the "*so-called*" proof against homosexuality was directed (as the Old Testament) to ritualistic worship.

But wait a minute... what about female same-sex relationships? We see women being mentioned for the first and only time in all of the verses allegedly mentioning homosexuality. This is another major point of fallacy for the validity of these verses being used against the LGBT+ community — female homosexuality. Let's take another look at verses through the female perspective:

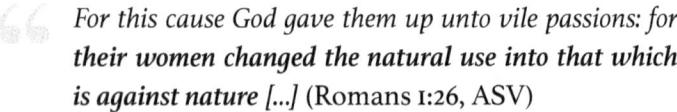

> *For this cause God gave them up unto vile passions: for* **their women changed the natural use into that which** **is against nature** *[...]* (Romans 1:26, ASV)

> *Because of this, God gave them over to shameful lusts.* **Even their women exchanged natural sexual relations** **for unnatural ones** *[...]* (Romans 1:26- 27, NIV)

Romans 1:26 is the first time we see women included in the context of alleged homosexuality, and even then, the choice of wording is ambiguous.

In the original Koine Greek, when Paul states that both men and women changed their natural "use," he uses the word χρῆσιν (chrēsin). Chrēsin is defined as a "function" and has a connotation of intimacy/acquaintance in certain contexts that allows us to assume we are safely using the word in sexual terms.

However, it is crucial to understand that in both Jewish and Greco-Roman patriarchal societies, the primary function of sex was procreation – vaginal penetration that resulted in children, in more explicit terms. Anal and oral sex were not common practice in the sex lives of the Romans. Prostitutes who would offer oral sex, for example, were often specialized in the act and were able to charge more for their services for that specific specialization[34].

Many scholars have written extensive academic journals that point out that Paul may not have meant to imply females having homosexual relations in verse 26. Instead, it is quite likely he is referring to the oral and anal sex practices of the priestesses[35].

This explanation would further clarify why Paul did not describe the female acts of his statement in as much detail as he did the male acts. It would have been common knowledge to the Romans that the "natural use" pertained to vaginal penetration.

BITE SIZED SUMMARY
Romans 1: 26-27

THE CHURCH'S CRUMBS: There can't be any mistake in interpreting this text. Paul explicitly lays out and condemns women who have slept with women and men who have slept with men. He even goes as far as to say that this kind of homosexual sex is unnatural.

SPILLING THE TEA: When reading any of Paul's letters to the communities of believers across the ancient world, you must be mindful of their culture and society. As with many of our previous cases, the interpretation of this text is a lack of contextualization. In this chapter, Paul describes idolatry, and in these particular verses, he is directly alluding to the many promiscuous practices of varying pagan cults of the Roman Empire.

These practices were a daily part of Roman life, and Paul's letter would immediately recall the imagery of the outrageous celebrations into their minds.

As for the use of what is natural vs. unnatural, the ancients had a very different idea of what constitutes as *natural* sex. Quite simply, if it wasn't vaginal penetration, it was considered unnatural.

1 Timothy 1:8-11

Timothy was one of apostle Paul's close mentees during his life ministry. In Acts 16, we see Paul stop by *Lystra* (located in modern-day Turkey) to pick up Timothy and take him along his journey across Asia Minor.

Scholars believe that at this point in life, Timothy was merely 16 years old but had a reputation as a good man among the community of believers in Lystra. In Acts, Paul is also mentioned to have circumcised Timothy for the Jews of the area to accept him, as Timothy's father was Greek. Remember, circumcision was seen as a mark of religious zeal to the Jewish people in those days.

Approximately 14-16 years later, we read Paul's first discovered letter to Timothy, who we find has been left in charge of the Ephesian community of believers in Paul's absence. If we do the math, Timothy is around 30 years old during this time.

This particular portion of text is another verse used against the LGBT+ community, let's see what Paul says to Timothy in a couple of translations:

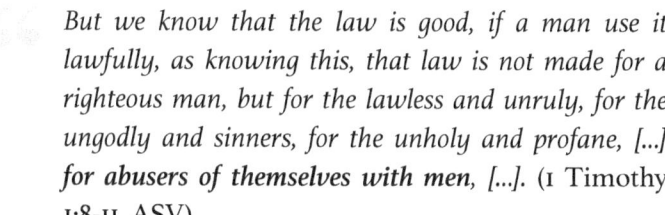

> *But we know that the law is good, if a man use it lawfully, as knowing this, that law is not made for a righteous man, but for the lawless and unruly, for the ungodly and sinners, for the unholy and profane, [...]* ***for abusers of themselves with men, [...].*** (1 Timothy 1:8-11, ASV)

> *We know that the law is good if one uses it properly. We also know that the law is made not for the righteous but for lawbreakers and rebels, the ungodly and sinful, the unholy and irreligious, [...]* ***for those practicing homosexuality, [...]*** *[...]* (1 Timothy 1:8-10, NIV)

Once again, here we find conflicting interpretations based on Paul's own coined term of *arsenokoites*. But, as we have already covered, the word has more than enough evidence to point towards a definition of pederasty.

Unfortunately, not much else on the matter is mentioned throughout this chapter, so we are left only to speculate and attempt a plausible interpretation. In this verse, Paul reminds us that the "Law" (or the law of Moses) was not established for the righteous (righteous being those saved in Christ) but for the lawless (the pagans).

It is also likely that Paul uses the term with Timothy to remind him of the immorality of pederasty, as it was common-place for the Greeks. At the time he received this letter, Timothy was of the age where an *eromenos* may have been procured, following tradition as a Greek man.

We can make another speculation through Paul's sequential train of logic as he wrote: first mentioning sexual immorality, then *arsenokoites* [or pederasty], and immediately following slavers, which, as we've learned, would also take part in the more abusive side of pederasty. They are all interrelated in nature,

In no other part of the Bible does Paul ever make mention of *arsenokoites* again.

BITE SIZED SUMMARY
1 Timothy 1: 8-11

THE CHURCH'S CRUMBS: Once again, Paul uses *arsenokoites* to condemn homosexuality. By direct association, he even calls those who practice it unrighteous.

SPILLING THE TEA: In his letter to Timothy, Paul is simply reinforcing the Law of Moses over the unrighteous. Since they don't accept salvation through Jesus, they must then live by the laws of the Old Testament to be saved.

As we covered in previous sections, his use of the word *arsenokoites* is used nowhere else in his letters other than 1 Corinthians and points to the meaning of pederasty. This would have specifically made sense to mention in his letter because Timothy was a Greek man who had reached the age where his peers were likely taking on their *eromenos* — boy lover. It was as if Paul was cautioning Timothy not to fall in line with the unrighteous practices of those that surrounded him.

The first time I analyzed all these texts and did some in-depth academic research, my immediate thought was, "EXCUSE ME?!"

It blew my mind that this information was logical, credible, and readily accessible if only people were interested in searching. So why, in all of these past centuries, haven't theologians simply said, "just kidding, we messed up," or at least made public that further study was necessary on the topic?

Then it hit me; it's not the first time the church has been wrong because of its overzealous desire to latch onto tradition and dogmas. The church has had a history of grave mistakes, and this time, it's no different.

Chapter 6

Oops, they did it again

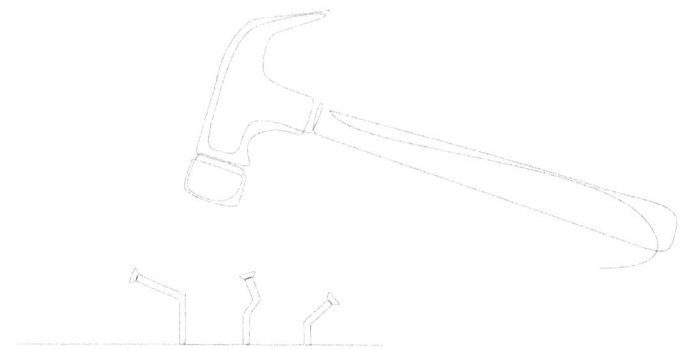

I t isn't the first time that the Church has misinterpreted Biblical text to the detriment of society. In fact, it has happened more often than not throughout human history, from issues as minor as how one should present themselves to issues as significant as racism.

Face it, the Church is composed of humans; humans are flawed. Furthermore, the tendency of Christians to be extraordinarily dogmatic and set in their ways creates a system in which any attempt at correcting faulty interpretations could take multiple generations to take hold. To most Christians, challenging any part of their beliefs is equated to an attack on the very essence of who they believe themselves to be, so there will always be those who resist change. This kind of fragile Christianity impedes any sort of progress.

Let's go over a few of these mistakes, starting with something small. One of my favorite memories of the past is drinking coffee with my parents around the kitchen island every morning. During that time, they would always share their stories about growing up, the obstacles they've faced, and how they overcame them. Hearing about how they grew up was a subject of particular interest that always left me in awe of how far they had come in their lives.

As I mentioned, my parents had always been part of pastoral families and had been heavily involved with church from the moment they had any concept of what it meant to have God in their lives. Being so deeply entrenched into religious culture, in a time when churches were deeply traditional, they faced strict rules that would raise eyebrows even in today's day and age.

Haircuts, jewelry, and pants, oh my!

Women in my mom's childhood church were not allowed to cut their hair unless it was to correct split ends. They were also forbidden to wear jewelry, aside from wedding rings, and could not wear jeans or pants. They were only allowed to wear skirts or dresses that needed to reach past their knees.

My mom would describe her trauma of having to bike around the neighborhood in a long-length skirt in the heat of the scorching Brazilian climate. Why was this a rule for the women of the church? Church officials would point to 1 Timothy 2:9, 1 Corinthians 11:5-6, and 1 Peter 3:3-4 for their instruction on this policy,

> *In like manner, that women adorn themselves in modest apparel, with shamefastness and sobriety; not with braided hair, and gold or pearls or costly raiment* (1 Timothy 2:9, ASV)

> *But every wife who prays or prophesies with her head uncovered dishonors her head, since it is the same as if her head were shaven. For if a wife will not cover her head, then she should cut her hair short. But since it is disgraceful for a wife to cut off her hair or shave her head, let her cover her head.* (1 Corinthians 11: 5-6, ESV)

> *Your beauty should not come from outward adornment, such as elaborate hairstyles and the wearing of gold jewelry or fine clothes. Rather, it should be that of your inner self, the unfading beauty of a gentle and quiet spirit, which is of great worth in God's sight.* (1 Peter 3:3-4, NIV)

We see another disregard to contextualization in Paul's letter to Timothy and Peter. Once again, Paul's recommendations for women to abstain from flashy jewelry and braided hair was not of a misogynistic nature (though Paul was very well known to make such comments in the context of his patriarchal society), but rather it was cautionary to preserve the approachability of the church while setting apart the community of believers from those around them. Additionally, short hairstyles were frequently attributed to prostitutes or enslaved people.

For the ancients, the use of opulent jewelry and complex hair designs was a woman's way of displaying social status[1] and wealth. In a faith whose roots were based on inclusivity and equality, the outward display of wealth would often leave people in those communities feeling inferior to their counterparts. The worship of God would then be distracted by self-comparison to others who could give more of their wealth to the community and would create the issues we would later see with the Catholic Church in the medieval ages, where wealth could allegedly determine salvation.

Likewise, women's adornment in the ancient past was often an issue of moral identification. Fashion in the Ancient Roman Empire were trends set by the prostitutes of the era, which were later toned down for the wear of the higher-class women. In fact, in many situations, they were almost indistinguishable. Kelly Olson analyzed the contemporary accounts of many moralists of the era and arrived at this conclusion[2],

> *It seems then that comparable kinds of feminine adornment could be used by both noblewomen and whores (certainly in varying degrees, but our authors do not acknowledge this). According to moralists, cosmetics and other adornment made a woman look seductive and served merely to invite male attention (the face of such*

*a woman, states Seneca, was proof of her shameless-
ness). Because, for the ancients, clothing and adornment
functioned as part of a moral system, and because
matronae and prostitutes employed similar types of
ornament, authors assert that they are often unable to
tell the difference between a whore and a respectable
woman.* (Olson, pg. 399)

So it seems, under the contextualization of the time, Paul's
guidance on the prohibition of jewelry served the community of
believers on multiple fronts. The warnings were meant to create
a safe space for believers on the grounds of inclusion, elimi-
nating an element of superiority complexes based on social
class, and distinguishing the faithful on moral grounds from
their contemporary counterparts in the prostitution industry.

This being said, jewelry did not serve the same purpose in
the modern age as it did in the ancient past. For the ancients,
jewelry was a means to communicate morality and display one's
social class. This practice of prohibition in churches, however,
lost its sway by the late 90s, though some more traditional estab-
lishments still observe it today. As for the strict ban on their use
of pants or shorts? An Old Testament verse answered the call:

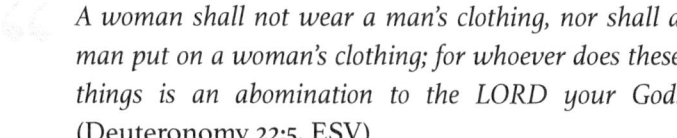

*A woman shall not wear a man's clothing, nor shall a
man put on a woman's clothing; for whoever does these
things is an abomination to the LORD your God.*
(Deuteronomy 22:5, ESV)

Clearly, in the minds of these church leaders,
pants/jeans/shorts were articles of clothing meant for men and
were inherently masculine in nature. How does this verse fit into
the ever-changing fashion we see in our society?

Before the 19th century (pre-1800s), the use of pants by

women was considered abhorrent, a symbol of masculinity. Yet, the style would change to make it commonplace for women to wear pants, jeans, and shorts in our modern age.

Where do we draw the line with the enforcement of these verses? History has taught us that it is necessary for a brave few to break norms and boundaries in order to influence societal change and trends. Are those few courageous individuals considered detestable before God, but suddenly it becomes acceptable when the rest of us adapt? We should seriously reconsider and hold ourselves accountable for this double standard.

In the last few centuries, millions have likely distanced themselves from the Church and from God because of such faulty interpretations. What did leaders hope to accomplish by being overzealous of such trivial matters? Was it worth gate-keeping people's souls from connecting with God over prohibitions of things as insignificant as pants and earrings?

My parents have told me countless stories of people shunned from the Church. I've heard so many stories of people forced to humiliate themselves before an entire congregation and beg for forgiveness because of a breach of these useless rules. When the Church prioritizes a set of rules over their love for people, we see a blatant violation of Jesus' direct order to love God and love people.

The "S" word Americans avoid.

We've reached an age where Christians, particularly American Christians, refuse to acknowledge the hurt, pain, and destruction caused by outdated religious beliefs. As I write this, conservative states push bills through the state legislature to attempt erasure of Black history in the country.

There is certain blindness in the Church of self-righteousness. Blindness that erroneously believes that it can do no harm because it represents God on earth. That opinion is *so* far from the truth. All we need to do is open a textbook for proof.

Slavery was once a hot-button topic for many around the world. Though the Bible was clear in John 3:16, that *all* those who believe in Him shall not perish but have eternal life, enslaved people were long considered property between the 16th and 17th centuries.

When the United States began its political debates over abolishing slavery, surprisingly, Christians would use the Bible to affirm their ownership of slaves.

> *Slaves, obey your earthly masters with respect and fear, and with sincerity of heart, just as you would obey Christ. Obey them not only to win their favor when their eye is on you, but as slaves of Christ, doing the will of God from your heart. Serve wholeheartedly, as if you were serving the Lord, not people, because you know that the Lord will reward each one for whatever good they do, whether they are slave or free.* (Ephesians 6:5-8, NIV)

As a side note, it's ironic that slave owners in the United States selectively chose to ignore the following verse as well:

> And masters, treat your slaves in the same way. Do not threaten them, since you know that he who is both their Master and yours is in heaven, and there is no favoritism with him. (Ephesians 6:9, NIV)

Other verses often used were Colossians 3:22 and Ephesians 2:18 in an attempt to secure their right to slave ownership. Slavery is a topic that many discuss as a major fallacy of the Bible. In this discussion, it is important to note a few things:

1. God hated oppression and championed in the aid of the oppressed.

- "The Lord is a stronghold for the oppressed..."
  Psalm 9
- "Learn to do good; seek justice; correct oppression..."
  Isaiah 1:17
- "Woe to those who decree iniquitous decrees, and the writers who keep writing oppression..." Isaiah 10:1-3

2. Slavery in the Old Testament among the Jews had strict laws regarding their treatment. Though God did not particularly condone it, he allowed it under the societal norms of that time. Still, in most of these circumstances, the slaves were allowed to go free after a specific time period and had the freedom to choose whether they wanted freedom or if they wished to continue in servitude.

Masters were sentenced to death if they killed a slave, and if they beat the slave and caused disabilities, the slave would be freed. Not that these rules made the practice any better, but here we see a stark contrast of slavery in the Old Testament vs. colonial times. Exodus 21 has a massive list regarding what was expected in the treatment of slaves that I encourage you to read for the purposes of comparison.

3. Slavery in the New Testament was highly commonplace. Nearly 10% of the Roman Empire's massive population was composed of slaves. Paul's instructions on treating one's slave with respect and kindness conformed to the societal norms

(Roman government's laws) of that time while condemning the mistreatment of the slaves.

There were also laws in which a slave could buy out their freedom under Roman regulations. Once again, starkly contrasted with the overwhelming majority of slaves in the US, which often lived and died on the fields under horrific conditions for the entirety of their lives.

This time in history was a shameful oversight and a tarnished stain in the Church's record of faults. Still, many prominent scholars and theologians of the time used scripture to support oppression, the exact opposite of what God had intended.

Bishop Stephen Elliot of Georgia (1806-1866) said this of slavery, "Never, in the history of the world, has there been such a rapid and effective missionary work [converting non-believers to Christianity] as the Christian church has performed in this land in connection with slavery."

The irony of such statements is that even when slaves were given Bibles, books like Exodus, which contained the story of the Israelites escaping their slavery under Egypt, were removed to prevent instilling ideas of rebellion[3]. Conversion to Christianity, it seemed, was only important when it suited them.

When questioned, modern-day Church leaders will likely claim that these verses on slavery were taken out of context for the times that they were written. They will affirm that these verses were maliciously used to support slavery.

So why wouldn't this same thought process be applied to the issue of homosexuality? Both communities have suffered from equal misinterpretation of Scripture. We can actually see more ambiguity in the interpretations of the gay-bashing verses than what we witness in the concise and direct verses on slavery.

On the other hand, if church leaders *do* affirm that the verses on slavery were not taken out of context, but rather, were allowed only to the society of those times, then again, why is the same not said about the gay-bashing verses?

Just as the Church often refuses to acknowledge the pain it caused to generations of black individuals, it will continue to do so for the LGBT+ community. It will take a brave few stand up and post their own "95 Theses" letters on the doors of the church, as Luther did to the Catholic Church.

Interracial Marriages

Stemming from the atrocities of slavery, interracial marriage was either unprotected by law or looked down upon in society for a long bleak period of our history. When *Gallup*, a global analytics firm, took a poll in 1958 asking US adults whether they approved of interracial marriage, only 4% stated they approved. In 2021, the poll was conducted once again[4] to reveal that this number had shot up to 94%. Unsurprisingly enough, the Church also had a hand in opposing interracial marriage through the use of Scripture to support its stance.

 Therefore do not give your daughters to their sons, neither take their daughters for your sons, and never seek their peace or prosperity, that you may be strong and eat the good of the land and leave it for an inheritance to your children forever. (Ezra 9:12, ESV)

You shall not intermarry with them, giving your daughters to their sons or taking their daughters for your sons, for they would turn away your sons from following me, to serve other gods. Then the anger of the

> *Lord would be kindled against you, and he would destroy you quickly.* (Deuteronomy 7:3-4, ESV)

> *As you saw the iron mixed with soft clay, so they will mix with one another in marriage, but they will not hold together, just as iron does not mix with clay.* (Daniel 2:43, ESV)

Again, the Church quickly applied verses taken out of context as law. In all these verses, the primary motive for the prohibition of marrying into different races/nations was not based on their skin. But, as mentioned previously, God had always wanted to set his people apart from the countries that surrounded them.

This exclusivity was not because of their race in and of itself but because of their beliefs. The purpose of these commandments was to keep people from marrying pagans who would bring in their own idol worship into a home that was consecrated [or set apart] for God. As we discover throughout the Old Testament, God will never share what is his with the likes of idols:

> *I am the Lord [Jehovah]; that is my name; my glory I give to no other, nor my praise to carved idols.* (Isaiah 42:8, ESV)

There is a continuance of this principle in the New Testament.

> *Do not be unequally yoked with unbelievers. For what partnership has righteousness with lawlessness? Or what fellowship has light with darkness?* (2 Corinthians 6:14, NIV)

It was never about race or mixing with people of other nations and cultures. It was always about bringing idols and foreign gods into the home and lives of those who were set apart and consecrated for God. Even so, we see "Christians" today who disapprove of interracial marriages.

In 2013, Tennesse Pastor Donnie Reagan of the 600-member Happy Valley Church preached a sermon rallying against bi-racial unions — receiving the approving *amens* from the congregation.

In the Youtube video floating around, he spares no senti-ments and says, "What white woman would want her baby to be a mulatto by a colored man?" He then goes on to say he is not a racist; he is just a man "who loves truths," using the Bible as his base.

Revenge against the Jews

Another big mistake the Church has committed in the past was instigating anti-Semitism. *What?! The Church?!* Yes. The Church. In fact, I would go as far as to say that the Church was respon-sible for planting the first seeds that would eventually surmount into the mass genocide that was the Holocaust.

Generally speaking, there has always been an uncomfortable tension between the Jewish and Christian faiths. Although the Bible states on multiple occasions that the Jewish people are God's chosen people, the sacrifice of Jesus opened that salvation up to everyone.

The point of contention has always come down to the iden-tity of the Messiah, or Savior. For those of Jewish faith, the belief remains that Jesus *was not* the Messiah and the Jewish people still await the coming of the Savior. For Christians, the belief is that Jesus *was* that Messiah and has resurrected from the dead, so Christians are now waiting for his second coming in the *Rapture*.

For centuries, this point of contention brought about a lot of blame against the Jewish people. Christians ultimately held them culpable for the death and rejection of Jesus as the Son of God. One particular verse that has often been used in such accusations comes to mind. When Jesus stood before *Pontius Pilate*, the Roman-appointed governor of Judaea, for judgment. He said to Pilate:

> *Jesus answered, My kingdom is not of this world: if my kingdom were of this world, then would my servants fight, that I should not be delivered to the Jews: but now is my kingdom not from hence.* (John 18:36, ASV)

Recent translations have clarified the meaning of this verse by changing *Jews* to *Jewish leaders*. Jesus was not generalizing the entire population of Jews but rather pointing to the Jewish leaders of that time who wished his death out of envy.

Unfortunately, this idea was not clarified in centuries past, and under these pretenses, the Jewish people became persecuted for political reasons through weaponized Scripture. These persecutions began during the Christian period of the Roman Empire, stemmed into the European Inquisitions in the Middle Ages, and all the way into the Holocaust[5].

Although most of Germany was Christian at the time of World War II, very few did anything to help Jews escape or stop the genocide. Like it or not, this misinterpretation and manipulation of Scripture has resulted in millions of lost innocent lives.

Separation of Church and State

There is a flawed belief that the Christian faith is the only thing that should dominate leadership in our governments. The logic follows that a leader who fears God is a leader whose nation will be blessed. These two verses come to mind:

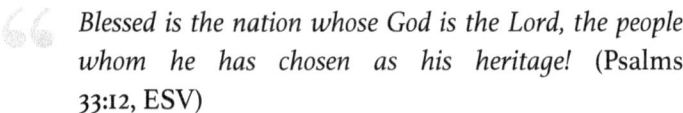

> *Blessed is the nation whose God is the Lord, the people whom he has chosen as his heritage!* (Psalms 33:12, ESV)

> *Righteousness exalts a nation, but sin is a reproach to any people.* (Proverbs 14:34, ESV)

But what exactly constitutes *righteousness*, and does that mean that religious ideals should ultimately drive our country? Righteousness is not something we can work towards; instead, it is given to us by faith.

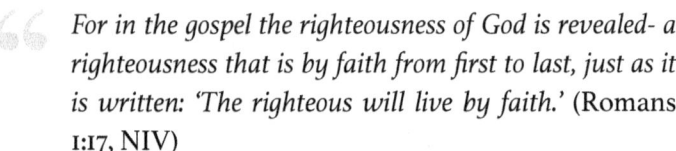

> *For in the gospel the righteousness of God is revealed- a righteousness that is by faith from first to last, just as it is written: 'The righteous will live by faith.'* (Romans 1:17, NIV)

> *This righteousness is given through faith in Jesus Christ to all who believe. There is no difference between Jew and Gentile.* (Romans 3:22)

In the Old Testament, the only path to righteousness was fulfilling God's laws as laid out by the Ten Commandments. With the sacrifice of Jesus, he satisfies those laws. Jesus became the ultimate sacrifice and the means to achieve any semblance of righteousness. His character and his nature were the models of a righteous life.

Now, if we know righteousness is found through Jesus, what does he say about religion and politics? Unsurprisingly enough, as a vehement opposer to the structures of power and oppression of the time, Jesus made it clear that his kingdom was not of this world (John 18:36). He further clarified his opinion on the separation of Church and state.

> *Then the Pharisees went out and laid plans to trap him in his words. They sent their disciples to him along with the Herodians. 'Teacher,' they said, 'we know that you are a man of integrity and that you teach the way of God in accordance with the truth. You aren't swayed by others, because you pay no attention to who they are. Tell us then, what is your opinion? Is it right to pay the imperial tax to Caesar or not?' But Jesus, knowing their evil intent, said, 'You hypocrites, why are you trying to trap me? Show me the coin used for paying the tax.' They brought him a denarius, and he asked them, 'Whose image is this? And whose inscription?' 'Caesar's,' they replied. Then he said to them, 'So give back to Caesar what is Caesar's, and to God what is God's.'* (Matthew 22:15-21, NIV)

This verse is particularly significant on many fronts. The *denarius* was a minted Roman coin used to pay one's taxes. On one side was an image of the emperor often accompanied by the

Latin equivalent of the word divine (it was common for the Roman emperors to deify themselves and demand worship as gods.) The religious leaders (Pharisees) tried to disprove Jesus as the Son of God by tricking him into saying they should pay their taxes, thus confirming to the people that he was in violation of the second commandment, which reads:

> *Thou shalt not make unto thee any graven image, or any likeness of anything that is in heaven above, or that is in the earth beneath, or that is in the water under the earth. Thou shalt not bow down thyself to them nor serve them* (Exodus 20:4-5, ASV)

Jesus' brilliant response established two distinct kingdoms, that of Caesar and that of God, and maintained that what belongs to Caesar stays with Caesar, and what belongs to God – the human soul – stays with God. Though we may currently be citizens of both, he notes a clear distinction we must observe. Here, Jesus clearly establishes a separation of Church and State.

Does that mean that our faith should not be part of governance by any means? In the purest essence of Christianity's virtues, I would say faith *could* be a great determinant of whether or not someone will be a righteous leader. However, the problem lies in human corruption.

Just as we have discussed that religion has been used in the past as a means to manipulate the masses, it continues to be used as such in modern-day politics. Simply put: a politician claims to be a Christian, claims to be a servant of God, claims to be of a particular political affiliation, and churchgoers across the nation immediately believe that this person is the right candidate for leadership; that this person is a man or woman of God. The Bible has countless warnings against this kind of behavior.

> *For such men are false apostles, deceitful workmen, disguising themselves as apostles of Christ. And no wonder, for even Satan disguises himself as an angel of light. So it is no surprise if his servants, also, disguise themselves as servants of righteousness. Their end will correspond to their deeds.* (2 Corinthians 11:13-15, ESV)

> *Not everyone who says to me, 'Lord, Lord,' will enter the kingdom of heaven, but the one who does the will of my Father who is in heaven. On that day many will say to me, 'Lord, Lord, did we not prophesy in your name, and cast out demons in your name, and do many mighty works in your name?' And then will I declare to them, 'I never knew you; depart from me, you workers of lawlessness.'* (Matthew 7:21-23, NIV)

So how exactly can we be sure if someone who claims to be a servant of Christ, a Christian, is the real deal? Luckily Jesus and Paul give us sound advice on the matter.

> *Beware of false prophets, who come to you in sheep's clothing but inwardly are ravenous wolves. **You will recognize them by their fruits.** Are grapes gathered from thornbushes, or figs from thistles? So, every healthy tree bears good fruit, but the diseased tree bears bad fruit. A healthy tree cannot bear bad fruit, nor can a diseased tree bear good fruit. Every tree that does not bear good fruit is cut down and thrown into the fire* (Matthew 7: 15-23, ESV)

> *Beloved, do not believe every spirit, **but test the spirits to see whether they are from God,** for many false*

prophets have gone out into the world. (1 John 4:1, ESV)

The test is simple. Hold up what the Scripture considers to be the fruits of the Spirit and fruits of righteousness against what the politician has done and said in the past.

> *The acts of the flesh are obvious: sexual immorality, impurity and debauchery; idolatry and witchcraft; hatred, discord, jealousy, fits of rage, selfish ambition, dissensions, factions and envy; drunkenness, orgies, and the like. I warn you, as I did before, that those who live like this will not inherit the kingdom of God. But the **fruit of the Spirit is love, joy, peace, forbearance, kindness, goodness, faithfulness, gentleness and self-control. Against such things there is no law.** [...]* (Galatians 5:19-26, NIV)

"But among you there must not be even a hint of sexual immorality, or of any kind of impurity, or of greed, because these are improper for God's holy people. Nor should there be obscenity, foolish talk or coarse joking, which are out of place, but rather thanksgiving. For of this you can be sure: No immoral, impure or greedy person—such a person is an idolater—has any inheritance in the kingdom of Christ and of God. Let no one deceive you with empty words, for because of such things God's wrath comes on those who are disobedient. Therefore do not be partners with them. [...]" (Ephesians 5:3-14, NIV)

When holding up a politician's behavior and policies to these verses, it becomes abundantly clear whether they are using their faith simply to manipulate people into voting for them or if they *actually* live out a genuine faith in God and Jesus Christ. Unfortunately, many in the Church have the audacity of saying a politician is a man of God when their track history directly contradicts everything Jesus and the Bible stand for.

The Abortion Conundrum

Abortion has long been a divisive issue among those of faith and those who advocate for women's rights. In all honesty, even I, at one point, considered myself pro-life until I started to do a bit more research into the matter. Among the verses that most Christians cling to in order to justify their beliefs, these are the most prominent:

> *Thou shall not murder.* (Exodus 20:13)

> *Before I formed you in the womb I knew you, before you were born I set you apart; I appointed you as a prophet to the nations.* (Jeremiah 1:5)

> *Children are a heritage from the LORD, offspring a reward from him. Like arrows in the hands of a warrior are children born in one's youth. Blessed is the man whose quiver is full of them. They will not be put to shame when they contend with their opponents in court.* (Psalms 127:3-5)

Remember how we discussed how one could interpret verses under different lenses? Though the first stated verse is quite literal in its meaning, the verses in Psalms and Jeremiah are clearly more poetic in nature.

In the same instance that these verses claim that our days have been set out before we were born, what's not to say that abortion had not been in God's plan? In fact, in the Old Testament, God gives explicit instruction on how to perform an abortion:

> *The priest shall bring her and have her stand before the Lord. Then he shall take some holy water in a clay jar and put some dust from the tabernacle floor into the water. After the priest has had the woman stand before the Lord, he shall loosen her hair and place in her hands the reminder-offering, the grain offering for jealousy, while he himself holds the bitter water that brings a curse. Then the priest shall put the woman under oath and say to her, "If no other man has had sexual relations with you and you have not gone astray and become impure while married to your husband, may this bitter water that brings a curse not harm you. But if you have gone astray while married to your husband and you have made yourself impure by having sexual relations with a man other than your husband"— here the priest is to put the woman under this curse—"may the Lord cause you to become a cursed among your people when he makes your womb miscarry and your abdomen swell. May this water that brings a curse enter your body so that your abdomen swells or your womb miscarries. Then the woman is to say, "Amen. So be it." The priest is to write these curses on a scroll and*

then wash them off into the bitter water. He shall make the woman drink the bitter water that brings a curse, and this water that brings a curse and causes bitter suffering will enter her. The priest is to take from her hands the grain offering for jealousy, wave it before the Lord and bring it to the altar. The priest is then to take a handful of the grain offering as a memorial offering and burn it on the altar; after that, he is to have the woman drink the water. If she has made herself impure and been unfaithful to her husband, this will be the result: When she is made to drink the water that brings a curse and causes bitter suffering, it will enter her, her abdomen will swell and her womb will miscarry, and she will become a curse. If, however, the woman has not made herself impure, but is clean, she will be cleared of guilt and will be able to have children. (Numbers 5:16-28, NIV)

Am I saying God condones abortions? Hard to say based on the text we just read. I believe God has plans of life for all of us, plans for good and not evil, as Jeremiah 29:11 promises. However, God is compassionate, and knows that different situations require different approaches.

Therefore let us not pass judgment on one another any longer, but rather decide never to put a stumbling block or hindrance in the way of a brother. I know and am persuaded in the Lord Jesus that nothing is unclean in itself, but it is unclean for anyone who thinks it unclean. (Romans 14:13-14, NIV)

We should not act as stumbling blocks for those who believe

that abortion is the only way forward for their lives. We are not God to determine whether women's decisions are justified or not and should not attempt to exert oppression based on beliefs that, quite honestly, are not clearly stated in the Bible.

Likewise, an argument can be made that the Bible plainly states that life is determined by first breath. Genesis 2:7 makes it clear that once God breaths in the breath of life, only then does man become a living soul. If we wish to get technical, a fetus' lungs are only fully developed at 24 weeks, in which a substance in the fetus' lungs "... allows the air sacs in the lungs to inflate — and keeps them from collapsing and sticking together when they deflate[6]." For perspective, 24 weeks is significantly past the deadline of current laws that allow abortions (12 weeks in most states).

Even with evidence in the Bible that contradicts the pro-life stance, the Church continues to terrorize those who opt to perform an abortion for one reason or another. Perhaps if we were truly pro-life, we would create a society that supports mothers enough to allow them the comfort to choose whether to proceed with birth. However, ironically enough, the same proponents for pro-life are the ones who vehemently oppose social welfare, universal healthcare, affordable birth control, facilitated adoptions for minority groups, and more.

Where has our compassion gone? What are we doing to better the social structures that could ultimately eliminate the need for abortions on a grander scale? The Church often tries to eliminate a symptom without treating the underlying cause.

Jesus himself predicted much of this in today's era,

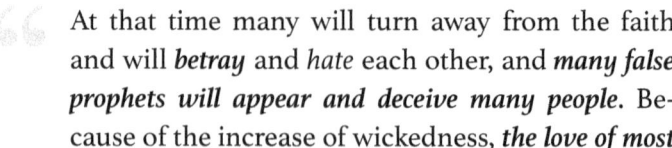

> At that time many will turn away from the faith and will *betray* and *hate* each other, and *many false prophets will appear and deceive many people.* Because of the increase of wickedness, *the love of most*

will grow cold, but the one who stands firm to the end will be saved. (Matthew 24:10-13, NIV)

Interestingly enough, this sounds a *lot* like Texas' attempt at instituting laws that allowed neighbors to claim a bounty if they would file a report to the state against any woman/healthcare provider who performed an abortion.

The Last Frontier

There are countless examples one could pull from history, many of which have been discussed in earlier chapters, where the Church has simply "*gotten it wrong.*" Ultimately, we must understand that the Church is a human institution and, by definition, intrinsically flawed.

The moment we come to terms with the fact that our version of Christianity has made mistakes and continues to make them, the quicker we can mobilize an attempt to try and fix it. Not within the institution itself but within *us*. All these mistakes were fervently supported by the Church at one point or another.

Pastors screamed from pulpits in support of slavery. Priests demanded the heads of the Jewish people. Theologians supported segregation and the prohibition of interracial marriage. Still, despite overwhelming support for maintaining these ideas in their contemporary times, they were ultimately revisited, restudied, and turned down.

It seems that for the LGBT+ community, we are one of the final unexplored frontiers in need of firm rediscovery by others in our faith. Although we may find and accept the truths within this book for ourselves, it is unlikely we will see a complete reformation of our right to be seen as human beings while older generations, still latched to traditions, continue to hold power.

I have hope in the Millennial, Gen Z, and future generations who have become more compassionate and tolerant. Maybe we won't see a complete reformation of the Church in our lifetime, but perhaps our children and grandchildren will live out the abundance of the change we make today.

Chapter 7

Where do we go from here?

Hello! I'm glad you've made it this far! I know a lot of this has been heavy subject matter to cover and quite overwhelming to process. Take your time, reread what you must, and do some research on your own — I highly encourage that when you Google these subjects, you research credible sources. Adding "academic journals" to the end of your search query can bring up some more credible search results. Burn down this "Facebook told me so" culture our parents and grandparents have latched on to. Knowledge is power, and misinformation is poison. The Bible itself warns us,

> *My people are destroyed for lack of knowledge; because you have rejected knowledge, I reject you from being a priest to me. And since you have forgotten the law of your God, I also will forget your children.* (Hosea 4:6, NIV)

So what *does* the Bible say about homosexuality? Honestly? Not much. It seems that it has never been an issue of great importance to address in the past. One thing the Bible *does* mention is that God doesn't make mistakes.

Science has recently disproven that there is a *specific* gay gene in our genetic makeup that would allow us to accurately predict homosexuality in individuals[1]. However, they *have* discovered that multiple patterns of genetic sequence seemed to overlap in those who do experience homosexual tendencies[2], but none in particular can be isolated to determine homosexuality.

So what exactly does this mean? Homosexuality is a much more intrinsic part of someone's genetic makeup than we have ever thought possible. If the composition of one particular marker had been identified, what's to stop doctors and scientists from genetically modifying said marker to avoid homosexuality in future generations? Instead, the much more complex patterns and systems that contribute to homosexuality are interwoven along the entirety of our genetic makeup.

To reaffirm bluntly, God does *not* make mistakes. Before you were even born, He knew *exactly* who you were going to be.

> *This God—his way is perfect; the word of the Lord proves true; he is a shield for all those who take refuge in him.* (Psalm 18:30, ESV)

> *And we know that for those who love God all things work together for good, for those who are called according to his purpose.* (Romans 8:28, ESV)

> *For you created my inmost being; you knit me together in my mother's womb. I praise you because I am fearfully and wonderfully made; your works are wonderful, I know that full well. My frame was not hidden from you when I was made in the secret place, when I was woven together in the depths of the earth. Your eyes saw my unformed body; all the days ordained for me were written in your book before one of them came to be.* (Psalm 139:13-16, NIV)

> *For I know the plans I have for you," declares the LORD, "plans to prosper you and not to harm you, plans to give you hope and a future.* (Jeremiah 29:11, NIV)

At this point, you're probably wondering: what now? What can we do with this information that could ever make a difference? If you're someone who, like me, has struggled to align their faith with their sexual identity, I hope this book gives you peace to know your worth. You are *not* a mistake. You are *not* an abomination. You are "*wonderfully and fearfully made*" just as you are.

If you are a parent, family member, or friend who approached this book with an open mind and can now see the mistakes you've made, I hope this book marks the start of a journey of healing. Heal your family, heal your friendships, heal your own heart with forgiveness for your past actions. You are human, and there is a path forward.

If you are a church leader who finds truth in these pages, you have a responsibility. You are the Luther we need to post truths on the doors of your community; the shepherd responsible for leading your flock to love the very outcast Jesus calls you to save.

I don't expect this book to receive much positive attention. I honestly expect the opposite. By writing this book, I'm attempting to post my own 95 *theses* on the doors of a centuries-old establishment. I'm calling out indoctrinated misinformation that spans hundreds of my lifetimes. This book represents a true *David and Goliath* scenario. But my most important priority and hope is that this book will stir you to "be the change" in the parameters of your own world.

If you find yourself rejected by a community of believers who were meant to love you, find a community that will. Your community doesn't have to be a church. Instead, your community could simply be another good friend who supports you as *you*.

As we learned from the ancient Church, Jesus never meant for the establishment of organized religion. Instead, he criticized the religious and scolded them for preaching what they did not live out.

Church does not have to be defined by the limits of a building. When you go out with friends for brunch and talk about the good things God has done in your life, that's church. When your story about how you overcame struggles and found yourself in God touches the life of another friend, that's church. When you call your friends over to hang around a bonfire and sing worship songs together, that's church. When you're hanging out with your best friend, and showing them love through a tough time, that's church. When you're out in public and buy lunch for a homeless person, that's church.

Throw aside these antiquated mindsets that you are only on God's good side if you're attending weekly church services. Your *life* is the ultimate act of worship to God. How you treat others, help others, and support others is *true* evangelism — a genuine reflection of God's love on Earth.

I felt worthless for a significant part of my life, like I was a mistake. No matter how hard I prayed or how much I tried, I felt like I was never living up to the full potential God had planned for me. The more I suppressed this part of me, the more depressed I became. Life seemed to be futile, and nothing I did felt like it would ever be good enough for God, for myself, or my family.

After countless hours of therapy, countless sleepless nights, and days and days of poring over scholarly journals and Biblical text, I was able to come to terms with the simple truth — God made me this way, and he did it for a reason.

I haven't been a part of a church community for years now, but I've built a community of my own: friends, who have become my chosen family, and many others who share the same faith. Straight, bi, lesbian, gay, and everything in between have become a part of my ministry and my immediate community of believers.

Whether you find yourself shunned from a community you were so deeply involved with, or if you've been abandoned by your own family and group of friends, I promise you one thing with the full certainty of my heart — God has *not* abandoned you. The same God you grew up singing worship songs to, the same one whose Bible stories you read, is the same one who is at the door of your heart, ready to make you whole again.

As I mentioned in the beginning, it took me an extremely long time to separate the hurt the Church had caused me from the genuine love of God. I wholeheartedly believe that the God preached on the pulpit on Sunday mornings is often not the fullness of the real God.

The God that the Church often portrays is a small fraction of the truth, corrupted, in part, by human bias. There is a journey ahead of you that will stretch out far beyond the four walls of a church. A journey that will take you to experience the fullness of a true God who wishes to be known by you.

I hope that the words of this book and the research I've presented can help start your journey of self-acceptance and understanding. You are not alone, and you will never be alone; remember that! There are countless resources available that you can explore with a community of like-minded queer Christians.

If you are a family member or a friend looking to understand this community of faith, I invite you to dive deep into the available resources out there. Websites like QChristian.org offer great starting points to continue your research.

Believe it or not, there are also amazing and affirming church communities that partner with the Gay Christian Network to provide a safe environment for LGBT+ individuals of faith. Surround yourself with people who have a passion for

God and who understand the assignment: that in the end, it's all about loving God and loving people.

If you find yourself in dangerous environments, I pray that God will show you a way out. I pray that He gives you the strength to endure the storm, and that the clouds will break overhead, to provide you with the means to leave whatever situation you're in. Don't be afraid to seek help from those you trust and love you for the person you are.

I urge you not to give up, not to give in, because your life is *so* tremendously valuable, *so* tremendously precious, regardless of whatever else you may have heard in your church, family, or community. Things will get better, and you will overcome!

A harsh lesson I had to learn in my own life was the ability to say no. Though I have always been big on family, their stubbornness to discuss a huge part of my life has led me to tough decisions. Though I love them with all my heart, boundaries needed to be established.

Unfortunately, the outcome was less of their overall involvement in my life. You will not convince people who are closed-minded in their ways. You may fantasize about the best possible outcomes, but you must understand that they may not come to fruition. All that's left to do is pick yourself up, affirm your worth (both in your own eyes and in the eyes of God), and move forward into the abundant life God has planned for you.

> You are *beautifully and wonderfully made*.
> You are *not* an abomination.
> You *are* a child of God.
> Your existence *is* valid.
> You *are* loved.
> You *are* free.

About the Author

Mitchell Kesller was born in Minas Gerais, Brazil, and later moved to Boston, MA. Raised Bostonian, he moved to Orlando, FL, fell in love with it, and refused to leave. Though Orlando is his homebase, you can also frequently find him traveling to Italy to explore more of the ancient and medieval history it holds. As such, he speaks English, Portuguese, and Italian.

A *Philosopher* in the word's original sense, Mitchell has never stopped chasing after wisdom and continued education. Though achieving two Bachelor's degrees in unrelated fields, his passion has always been to thoroughly study ancient history and religious topics. His literary tastes fall under topics of Greek mythology, fantasy, sci-fi, and philosophy.

He and his fiancé, Daniel, currently live in Orlando. When they aren't traveling abroad, they enjoy exploring the city for its different restaurants and can often be spotted hanging out in the region's many theme parks. As avid Harry Potter fans, Mitchell is a Ravenclaw while Daniel is a Slytherin; they are both strong in the force within the Star Wars fandom.

Both Mitchell and Daniel believe in a world where those of faith can find comfort in who they are and continuously contribute their tithes to organizations like the *Trevor Project,* which support the rights and well-being of the LGBT+ community.

Readers are encouraged to share their stories by email!
hello@mitchellkesller.com
www.mitchellkesller.com

instagram.com/mitchellkesller

Notes

1. A Battle Within

1. "MAHATMA GANDHI SAYS HE BELIEVES IN CHRIST BUT NOT CHRISTIANITY: News: The Harvard Crimson." News | The Harvard Crimson.

2. Ancient History

1. Pavlovitz, John. "Remember, the Bible Never Mentions a Building Called 'Church'." RELEVANT.
2. Dr Sophie Lunn-Rockliffe, "History - Ancient History in Depth: Christianity and the Roman Empire," BBC, February 17, 2011
3. Frank Dunkle, David Cobb. "Paganism In Christianity." United Church of God.
4. "In What Language Was the Bible First Written?" Biblica. October 13, 2020.
5. "The Martin Luther Bible Translation." Christian History for Everyman.
6. Behance, Inc. "Creative Bad Habits: Treading The Path of Least Resistance." Adobe 99U. February 27, 2019.
7. Mcleod, Saul. "Obedience to Authority." Obedience to Authority | Simply Psychology.

3. The B-I-B-L-E

1. OUPAcademic. "The Challenges of Translating Ancient Greek." YouTube. November 11, 2013.
2. Ebeling, D. J. R. (n.d.). *Recent archaeological discoveries at Hazor.* Recent Archaeological Discoveries at Hazor | Bible Interp. Retrieved February 9, 2022, from https://bibleinterp.arizona.edu/articles/Hazor_Ebeling
3. Hagerty, B. B. (2011, August 9). *Evangelicals question the existence of adam and eve.* NPR. Retrieved February 9, 2022, from https://www.npr.org/2011/08/09/138957812/evangelicals-question-the-existence-of-adam-and-eve

4. Who is God, Anyway?

1. Keep, Lennlee. "A Flood of Myths and Stories." PBS.
2. Blaxland, B., & Dorey, F. (2020, March 4). *The first migrations out of Africa.* The First Migrations out of Africa. Retrieved February 9, 2022, from https://australian.museum/learn/science/human-evolution/the-first-migra-tions-out-of-africa/
3. Yehuda, R., & Lehrner, A. (2018). Intergenerational transmission of trauma effects: putative role of epigenetic mechanisms. *World psychiatry : official journal of the World Psychiatric Association (WPA), 17*(3), 243–257. https://doi.org/10.1002/wps.20568

5. The Gay Bashers

1. Pirkei Avos 1:5 "Chapter of the Fathers" from a Judaic compilation of ethical maxims. Earliest commentary of this theory made by Rabbeinu Yona.
2. Beckman, G. (2013). Foreigners in the Ancient Near East. Journal of the American Oriental Society, 133(2), 203. doi:10.7817/jameroriesoci.133.2.0203
3. Klotz, I. M. (1988). The Chemical Death of Lots Wife: Discussion Paper. Journal of the Royal Society of Medicine, 81(7), 397-398. doi:10.1177/014107688808100712
4. Killing the Canaanites: A Response to the New Atheism's "Divine Genocide" Claims. (n.d.). Retrieved from https://www.equip.org/article/killing-the-canaanites/
5. See the Papyrus Chester Beatty III recto (BM10683) from about 1175 BC as referenced in Lise Manniche, Sexual Life in Ancient Egypt (London: Routledge, 1987), 100.
6. Moloch. (n.d.). Retrieved from https://www.britannica.com/topic/Moloch-ancient-god
7. Mark S. Smith, trans. Ugaritic Narrative Poetry, ed. Simon B. Parker (Atlanta: Society of Biblical Literature, 1997), 148.
8. Stephanie Dalley, "Erra and Ishum IV," Myths from Mesopotamia (Oxford: Oxford University, 1989), 305.
9. Abomination. (n.d.). Retrieved from https://www.dictionary.com/browse/abomination
10. Will & Testament: Have you committed an "abomination" today? (n.d.). Retrieved from https://www.bbc.co.uk/blogs/ni/2008/06/have_you_commit-ted_an_abominat.html
11. Acts 21-23
12. Acts 9
13. 1 Corinthians 9:1

14. First printed Bible in English - The British Library. (n.d.). Retrieved from https://www.bl.uk/learning/timeline/item101093.html#:~:text=William Tyndale's Bible was the,by law conducted in Latin.

15. Harvard University Department of the Classics - Dictionaries. (n.d.). Retrieved from https://classics.fas.harvard.edu/dictionaries

16. H.S. Jones and J.E. Powell, Thucydidis historiae, 2 vols., Oxford: Clarendon Press, 1:1942 (1st edn. rev.); 2:1942 (2nd edn. rev.) (repr. 1:1970; 2:1967) Retrieved from: http://stephanus.tlg.uci.edu/Iris/Cite?0003:001:206523

17. J. Burnet, Platonis opera, vol. 4, Oxford: Clarendon Press, 1902 (repr. 1968): St II.327a-621d. Retrieved from: http://stephanus.tlg.uci.edu/Iris/Cite?0059:030:520899

18. H.S. Jones and J.E. Powell, Thucydidis historiae, 2 vols., Oxford: Clarendon Press, 1:1942 (1st edn. rev.); 2:1942 (2nd edn. rev.) (repr. 1:1970; 2:1967) Retrieved from: http://stephanus.tlg.uci.edu/Iris/Cite?0003:001:798384

19. Aristotle, Nicomachean Ethics H. Rackham, Ed. Aristotle, Nicomachean Ethics, bekker page 1150a, bekker line 20. (n.d.). Retrieved November 3, 2021, from http://data.perseus.org/citations/urn:cts:greekLit:tlg0086.tlg010.perseus-eng1:1150a.20.

20. Plato, Republic. Plato, Republic, Book 3, section 398e. (n.d.). Retrieved November 3, 2021, from http://data.perseus.org/citations/urn:cts:greekLit:tlg0059.tlg030.perseus-eng1:3.398e.

21. Jacoby, D. (2020, November 9). Malakoi, arsenokoitai, and homosexuality. Douglas Jacoby. Retrieved November 3, 2021, from https://www.douglasjacoby.com/qa-1510/?gclid=Cj0KCQjw5oiMBhDtARIsAJioqk2wYWLeVrFWx5oU2ppLObqi6tfLtecnzJtp8SuO7GvIHuVrmdSaFewaAjouEALw_wcB.

22. Forbes, M. (2021, August 24). Prostitution in Ancient Greece and Rome. TheCollector. Retrieved November 3, 2021, from https://www.thecollector.com/prostitution-ancient-greece-rome/

23. Mason, E., & Cartledge, P. (2021, September 17). What was pederasty in Ancient Greece? History Extra Podcast - Everything you wanted to know about Ancient Greece, but were afraid to ask (part 2). Retrieved November 4, 2021, from https://www.historyextra.com/period/ancient-greece/pederasty-homosexuality-ancient-greece-boys-sparta-girls-plato-sappho-consent/.

24. Miller, J. E. (1997). Response: Pederasty and romans 1:27:a response to Mark Smith. Journal of the American Academy of Religion, 65(4), 861–866. https://doi.org/10.1093/jaarel/65.4.861

25. Garcia, B. (2022, January 13). Venus. World History Encyclopedia. Retrieved January 14, 2022, from https://www.worldhistory.org/venus/

26. F., B. S. G. (2014). Beliefs, rituals, and symbols of ancient greece & rome. Cavendish Square Publishing.

27. Macrobius, The Saturnalia (trans. Percival Vaughan Davies; New York: Columbia University Press, 1969), 214 (3.8.2–3).

28. Whelan, E. (2021, June 28). Megalesia: Rome's shocking religious festival. Classical Wisdom Weekly. Retrieved January 14, 2022, from https://classicalwisdom.com/culture/traditions/megalesia-romes-shocking-religious-festival/

29. Pachis, P. (2020). Rites of the day of blood (dies sanguinis) in the Graeco-roman cult of Cybele and Attis. Journal of Cognitive Historiography, 5(1-2), 37–55. https://doi.org/10.1558/jch.39915

30. Roller, L. E. 1999. In Search of God of The Mother. The Cult of Anatolian Cybele. Berkeley and London: University of California Press.

31. Cult of isis. Ancient Rome History at UNRV.com - Cult of Isis . (n.d.). Retrieved January 15, 2022, from https://www.unrv.com/culture/isis.php

32. Spence, R. B. (2020, August 8). The Isis cult-the story of the Egyptian goddess. The Great Courses Daily. Retrieved January 15, 2022, from https://www.thegreatcoursesdaily.com/the-isis-cult-the-story-of-the-egyptian-goddess/

33. OSGOOD, J. (2008). CAESAR AND NICOMEDES. *The Classical Quarterly, 58*(2), 687-691. doi:10.1017/S0009838808000785

34. Tyner, K. M. (2015). Roman Social-Sexual Interactions: A critical examination of limitations of Roman sexuality (thesis).

35. Townsley, J. (2011). Paul, the goddess religions, and queer sects: Romans 1:23—28. Journal of Biblical Literature, 130(4), 707. https://doi.org/10.2307/23488275

6. Oops, they did it again

1. Bartman, E. (2001). Hair and the Artifice of Roman Female Adornment. *American Journal of Archaeology, 105*(1), 1–25. https://doi.org/10.2307/507324

2. Bartman, E. (2001). Hair and the Artifice of Roman Female Adornment. *American Journal of Archaeology, 105*(1), 1–25. https://doi.org/10.2307/507324

3. Zauzmer, J. (2021, October 27). The New Museum of the Bible confronts the challenge of presenting slavery and the confederacy. The Washington Post. Retrieved March 3, 2022, from https://www.washingtonpost.com/news/acts-of-faith/wp/2017/11/16/the-new-museum-of-the-bible-confronts-the-challenge-of-presenting-slavery-and-the-confederacy/

4. McCarthy, J. (2021, November 20). U.S. approval of interracial marriage at new high of 94%. Gallup.com. Retrieved February 7, 2022, from https://news.gallup.com/poll/354638/approval-interracial-marriage-new-high.aspx

5. Sloyan, G. S. (n.d.). Christian persecution of Jews over the centuries. United States holocaust memorial museum. Retrieved February 7, 2022, from https://www.ushmm.org/research/about-the-mandel-center/initiatives/ethics-religion-holocaust/articles-and-resources/christian-persecu-

tion-of-jews-over-the-centuries/christian-persecution-of-jews-over-the-centuries

6. Mayo Foundation for Medical Education and Research. (2020, June 30). Fetal development: What happens during the 2nd trimester? Mayo Clinic. Retrieved February 7, 2022, from https://www.mayoclinic.org/healthy-lifestyle/pregnancy-week-by-week/in-depth/fetal-development/art-20046151#:~:text=Week%2026%3A%20Baby's%20lungs%20develop,sticking%20together%20when%20they%20deflate.

7. Where do we go from here?

1. Lambert, J. (2019, August 29). *No 'gay gene': Massive study homes in on genetic basis of human sexuality*. Nature News. Retrieved March 6, 2022, from https://www.nature.com/articles/d41586-019-02585-6

2. Zietsch, B. (2019, August 30). *'gay gene' search reveals not one but many – and no way to predict sexuality*. UQ News. Retrieved March 6, 2022, from https://www.uq.edu.au/news/article/2019/08/gay-gene%E2%80%99-search-reveals-not-one-many-%E2%80%93-and-no-way-predict-sexuality

Additional References

Cecil, W. (n.d.). *Greek language and civilization - Youtube*. Retrieved March 16, 2021, from https://www.youtube.com/watch?v=l5Iz-IGHWLdo.

Goff, M. (n.d.). *First Printed Bible in English*. The British Library - The British Library. Retrieved March 16, 2021, from https://www.bl.uk/learning/timeline/item101093.html#:~:text=William.

London, R. (2019, February 28). *Masculinity in Ancient Greece*. The Courtauldian. Retrieved November 4, 2021, from https://www.-courtauldian.com/single-post/2019/02/28/masculinity-in-ancient-greece.

Miller, J. H. (n.d.). *The Rhetoric of Gay Christians: Matthew ... - UNLV Libraries*. Retrieved March 13, 2021, from https://digi-talscholarship.unlv.edu/cgi/viewcontent.cgi?article=3123&con-text=thesesdissertations.

Additional References

Scroggs, R. (n.d.). *What the Bible says - does the Bible not oppose homosexuality? | assault on gay america | frontline*. PBS. Retrieved November 3, 2021, from https://www.pbs.org/wgbh/pages/frontline/shows/assault/bible/doesnotoppose.html.